SIMULATED DREAMS

New Directions in Anthropology

General Editor: Jacqueline Waldren, *Sub-Faculty of Social Anthropology, University of Oxford*

SIMULATED DREAMS

Israeli Youth and Virtual Zionism

Haim Hazan

Berghahn Books
NEW YORK • OXFORD

First published in 2001 by
Berghahn Books

www.berghahnbooks.com

Library of Congress Cataloging-in-Publication Data

Hazan, Haim.
    Simulated dreams : Israeli youth and virtual Zionism / Haim Hazan.
        p. cm. – (New directions in anthropology : v. 14)
    Includes bibliographical references (p.) and index.
    ISBN 1-57181-821-9
        1. National characteristics, Israel. 2. Zionism. 3. Jews–Israel–
Identity. 4. Israel–Social conditions–20th century. 5. Memory–Social
aspects. 6. Jewish youth–Israel–Attitudes. 7. Popular culture–Israel.
I. Title. II. Series.

DS113.3 .H29 2001
956.9405–dc21   2001025783

British Library Cataloguing in Publication Data
A catalogue record for this book is available from
the British Library.

CONTENTS

Contents

Acknowledgments

This book is about representations of the rendezvous between codes of Zionist nationalism, globalization, and youth. The playful struggle between these cultural protagonists is staged in the public theater of the media, and *Simulated Dreams* offers the spectator-reader a seat for anthropological viewing of this show. The six-act play unfolded in this text is the result of a research effort in various channels, and the responsibility for their linkage, as well as to the ensuing arguments and conclusions drawn, are mine and mine alone. However, my gratitude is extended to those who assisted and encouraged me in the preparation of the manuscript: Professors Barbara Kirshenblatt-Gimblett, Jean and John Comaroff, Emanual Marx, Hannah Herzog, Michal Bodmann, and Gershon Shafir, who offered insightful comments and illuminating ideas. Thanks also to Dr. Aviad Raz, who contributed to the editing of the text, particularly to chapter 2, and Ms. Irit Dekel-Tsur, whose helpful notes were most welcome. I am greatly appreciative of the attentive care taken by the staff of Berghahn Books to ensure the fine production of the book.

PROLOGUE

The return of the prodigal son to his fatherland has been the generative myth upon which the Zionist claim for and enterprise of homecoming are edified. The motif of the wandering Jew who terminates his travels in the sanctified land of Israel and is thus transformed from a nomad to a settler is the core theme in the master narrative of that passage. The paragon of that pilgrimage, its justification and the bearer of its cross of sacrifice and redemption, is the archetype of the newly born, indigenous Israeli Jew who supposedly emerged from nowhere, drawing his strength and might from the elements of his old-new naturalized homeland.

This image was epitomized in the construction of the fine figure of the young warrior-cum-pioneer whose collective memory did not extend beyond the historical horizons of his land. Born and bred on constitutive myths of nation building and national exceptionalism, the youthful protagonist of the Zionist project had to deal with the dilemma of assuming responsibility for life and death without the corresponding authority of political and ideological leadership. This was previously reserved for and maintained by the oligarchy of Zionist elders who held the reigns of both cultural hegemony and organizational dominance. In time, the young cohort of yesterday have become the elders of today, and their own offspring are exposed to the continuous endeavor of engineering collective selves.

However, history is ambushing myth, and changes in the spirit of the times spell transformations in identity, priorities, and world-view. Thus, the question of the dynamic relationship between the living experience of the young and the mythical framework and formulae imposed on them becomes a prominent issue in the understanding of contemporary society. *Simulated Dreams* is an attempt to generate an ethnographically informed discourse pertaining to the Zionist case of that interplay between myth and reality in the lives of young people.

I am interested in the concept of youth for its dialectical nature. As the national progeny, "youth" is subjected to extensive socialization; at the same time, youth is characterized by its state of moratorium, a stage of permitted experimentation and expected rebellion. In other words, youth is a life stage in which the forces of collectivism and individualism most blatantly meet (and touch swords). As consumers, young people are the carriers of global culture; yet they also bring to this consumption their own cultural stamp. Israeli youth is a mixture of the local and the global, the Israeli and the Western, the cosmopolitan, the cool. Furthermore, as the age-group most conspicuously targeted by a host of "images of identity," postmodern Israeli youth is both simulation and reality.

In this book I focus on several major simulations featuring Israeli youth and Zionism. I draw for this purpose on a selection from my recent ethnographic work, which is reinterpreted here in a new framework. The guided tour we are about to take is a multisite, critical ethnography of a contrived "heritage zone" where Zionism and Israeli youth meet. This heritage zone includes youth films, TV war shows and Holocaust tours, poor neighborhoods and political funerals. A glimpse into the upcoming program can be gained by paying a brief visit to the campus of my own university—Tel-Aviv University in Israel.

Any ordinary university serves as both an institution of learning and a cultural device structuring age and controlling the admission of the young into adult society. The symbolic provisions offered by the university cater to a double-edged experience of both freedom and rules, intellectual individualism and collective exams. The campus of Tel-Aviv University is no exception to this duality. At the heart of the campus, straddling the departments of the humanities and the exact sciences, there is a striking arrangement of non-academic structures. The original component of this group of three is the Museum of the Jewish diaspora—an achronological permanent exhibition of mostly non-authentic items and a virtual display of Jewish existence in exile. Next to the museum lies a memorial pit for fallen Israeli soldiers. The symbolic juxtaposition between the two monuments is self-evident. The virtual museum casts its shadow onto ultimate authenticity: death in battle, the sanctity of the Zionist ethos. Finally, an imposing synagogue verges on the pit, overlooking both the memorial and the Holocaust museum. The result could be described as a threefold national narrative of calamity, death, and resurrection.

However, the synagogue is not a conventional Jewish house of prayer. Split into two equal scroll-like cylinders, the building is designed to project and reflect the spiritual essence of Orthodox Judaism alongside its spiritual inspirations on other faiths and creeds. Furthermore, the building itself, designed by Swiss architect Mario Botta, is coated with Italian stone and strongly resembles a Catholic church by the same architect in Evry, France.

The bottom line of this brief semiotic analysis is that the "heritage zone" in the center of the Tel-Aviv campus is a bricolage. Like youth, its designated audience, this zone represents the dialectics of the local and the global, the familiar and the foreign, the unique and the universal. In the heritage zone, the themes of the Holocaust, the fallen Israeli soldiers and Jewish religion—all hinging on real historical events—are reconstructed and assembled in a manner that replaces reality with a simulation. This book, then, is not about youth culture per se, nor is it about inter-generational relations. Even though young people are the readers and performers of the cultural texts to be examined here, the source of these texts (like the source of the "heritage zone") is the world of adults. The reader should remain alert to the reproduction of power that takes place in the following chapters, and judge for him or herself whether the reality behind the simulation is, ultimately, the usurpation of youth by middle-age society.

This assumption is not merely a reflection of some intergenerational cleavage, but a key cue for a critical reading of Israeli culture. It is no coincidence that the figure of the proverbial *Sabra*—the common icon of traditional Zionism—is customarily depicted as a defiant, cheeky-looking, slovenly, scout-attired, boisterous youth. Add to that similar major cultural idioms ingrained in abundant literature, cinema, plastic arts, and, most importantly, school curricular agenda promoting the trope of the eternally youthful indigenous or pseudo-indigenous Israeli. Israeli society, whose investments in reproductive technologies, prenatal tests, and child-rearing expenditures are unprecedented in the Western world, indicates an unequivocal commitment, even obsession, with its young. Patterns of adult behavior such as sing-alongs, speech forms, rituals of collectivity, and playful gestures, are all manifestations of the prevalence of childlike manner among Israelis. Youthfulness and its rhetorics are thus the generative language of Israeli cultural identity.

It produces infantile properties of authoritarianism, blended with playfulness and pedagogic dramaturgical presentations plotted as mythical scriptures accompanying socialization. The purpose—latent or explicit —of this cultural agenda could be explicated in terms of preparation for the ultimate in national identification, for example, army service and its possible aftermath—death at an early age. The construction of the childlike native is thus edified on the notion of, and the need for, unquestionable sacrifice modeled on the binding of the compliant child Isaac. Even though the perseverance of this total expectation is tempered with multicultural experience and postmodern revelry, the ethos of the fearless, intrepid child whose fighting spirit is unshaken by his denied morality is still widely fostered and prevalent. Hence, youth is much more than an age category or a generational stratum; it is an encapsulated epoch symbolically perfected in the immortal Zionist child hero.

This book is dedicated to the discovery of some of the expression of that core trope of Zionism within the cultural context of global representations. If, as suggested, the images of Israeli youth are viable and vibrant, then the following narratives are bound to testify to their embedded transitional, as well as invariant, qualities.

For Mercia,
A woman of valor

INTRODUCTION
Simulated Dreams

⟨∞⟩

*I*n the course of conducting fieldwork in one of Israel's poor neighborhoods undergoing "renewal," I heard a local version of a children's story told in a day care center for the elderly. The story, written by famous Israeli poet Dan Pagis, is called "The Disguised Egg." It recounts the adventures of an egg that becomes fed up with its eggy identity and ventures to seek its fortune in other round forms—a balloon, an apple, a ball, and other oval-shaped objects. Having found all these "disguises" unsatisfactory, the egg concludes that it cannot change into something else. It returns with relief to its original egg shape and hatches a chick.

The story, a classic of children's literature in Hebrew, was assigned as reading for an elderly group of women, a practice common in literacy classes for new immigrants. The interpretation offered by the elderly readers, however, was unique. Readers offered almost identical explanations as to why the story had struck a chord with them. They saw the tale as a post-colonial allegory of their own identity. Like the egg, they had embarked on a long journey, having immigrated to Israel from their countries of origin, whose culture they had internalized. In Israel they had passed through various phases, at each of which an attempt had been made to transform their primordial identity into something else. Immigrants from all countries were expected to submerge themselves in the melting pot of the new Israeli society, changing their diaspora-sounding family names into Hebrew names,

1

expunging traditional languages, class systems, occupations, and social relationships. This sweeping project was carried out by an Ashkenazi establishment. The captivating dream of a new and homogeneous Israel was therefore also reproducing and reenforcing the already-existing ethnic hierarchy of the pre-state community. The elderly Sephardi women of the center could remember, like many other immigrants, how in transit camps for immigrants they had been expected to become Israelis, and later on—in the neighborhood—how others had tried to impart them with a foreign culture. With hindsight, they claimed that their true selves were to be found only in their origins, in their undisguised ethnic affiliations. Some went even further in developing this thesis, remarking that only once it had accepted itself for what it was could the egg become fertile. In their case, too, only once they had resigned themselves to what they were, not through necessity but by choice, could they become meaningful to their grandchildren.

The elderly Sephardi women articulated, in reaction to the Ashkenazi text assigned to them, what is now becoming a common Israeli condition—a gradual shift from a collectivist to a multicultural society, a shift from the monolingual to the multivocal and from the colonial to the post-colonial. In articulating this, however, the elderly Sephardi women spoke from the fringes of their community. Although a large and active day center had been opened for the elderly of the neighborhood, their status within the community was marginal. They were seen as representatives of the traditional, ethnic neighborhood identity, and many of them received welfare support, which perpetuated the neighborhood's stigma of poverty. This predicament resembled that of contemporary voices of Sephardi intellectuals: it was the wisdom of the fringes—and of old age—that enabled the elderly readers to be critical of appearances, captivating as they might be, and search for the "thing in itself."

Generally speaking, historians of the Israeli collectivity have long concerned themselves with the egg rather than its disguises. That is, they have taken for granted the essence and importance of the Israeli collectivity, the given fact of its egginess, and paid less attention to the continuous boundary work involved in the shaping of that collectivity. In dealing with Israeli collective memory, the mainstream social scientific stance has been similarly constructive, rather than de-constructive. Much sociological work has been dedicated to the collective processes of commemoration; much less to social amnesia. In the same vein, ideology has been taken as part and parcel of the efforts required for nation building. Alternative and contesting versions—those of the elderly, the Sephardi, adolescents, the diaspora Jews, the Palestinians—have been (have had to be) subjected to the master commemorative narrative of the Israeli (hence, Jewish, Zionist, Ashkenazi, adult) collectivity.

This book looks at the myths of Israeli society, particularly within youth culture, and how they stand up to their post-colonial reality. It opens a window to contemporary Israel through some of its key ideological texts, media events, and social dramas. Its ethnographic examples cover popular films and TV programs, media events, actualities turned into media events (Prime Minister Yitzhak Rabin's assassination), and social dramas such as those encapsulated in youth delegations to concentration camps or in urban "rehabilitation neighborhoods." The amalgamation of such a varied group of cases is made possible by analyzing their common themes.

First, what is being studied here is a textual corpus: the dynamic *writing and editing* of Israeli culture as it is conducted in TV, film, news editions, educational handbooks and other "national texts of identity" designed for youth. Second, these texts have been selected so as to represent important sites of memory. The Holocaust; the Sephardi, deprived neighborhood; the media events of the Gulf War and of Rabin's assassination; are all key locations for a contemporary narrating of the Israeli story. Third, these texts are all what anthropologists call "liminal": they capture a certain process of transmutation. The imaginary (cinematic, electronic, media-based) as well as the actual (war, assassination) are mixed in them. All these texts possess the quality of merging myth and history. This liminality of the texts has facilitated, for example, the emergence of the slain Prime Minister Rabin as an "immortal" national father, the emergence of youth delegations to concentration camps as national rites of initiation, or the dramatic enactment of a cleansed "community" in an urban, deprived area.

All these cases are connected in some way to Israeli youth. They provide a key not only to how Israeli youth remembers, but—and no less important—how they are made to unlearn and forget. Commemoration always involves amnesia as well as remembering (Anderson 1993). Furthermore, by highlighting several key events for contemporary youth in Israel—the Gulf War, Rabin's assassination, Holocaust delegations—I hope to show the local features of that age-group.

The narratives of our assigned reading are common to Israeli culture. These narratives retell, for example, the story of how the few

3

struggle against the many (Holocaust delegations); how the European civilization of "First Israel" collides with the "tribal East" of "Second Israel" (the deprived neighborhood); and how individuals are forged into a nation-in-arms (the "group film," *Late Summer Blues*). These narratives, like myths in general, hinge on binary oppositions: the few and the many, self and other, West and East, individual and collectivity. These are basic, indeed universal, premises of human culture. It is the fundamental and universal nature of myth to facilitate not only the mutual explication of such dichotomies, but also their fusion. Myths have the power to reconcile irreducible opposites. Individuals, therefore, can be enlisted, West and East can be brought together, and the dead can live again (if only through symbolic immortality). In the Israeli case, this reconciliation of opposites has been mediated through and propelled by particular national ideologies such as Zionist socialism, Israeli militarism, and Jewish fundamentalism.

The five chapters of the book illustrate, through their choice of texts, how such myths subjugate the ethos of individuality—and how individuals (or social groups) have more recently begun to deconstruct such myths. The first part of the argument (the hegemonic power of myths) has been the current focus of an upsurge of social scientific literature regarding Israeli collective memory (e.g., Ben Ari and Bilu 1997; Ben-Yehuda 1995; Zerubavel 1995). The second, complementary part of the argument—how individuals and social groups can deconstruct such myths—is, in contrast, the main theoretical perspective of this study.

Myths and Simulations

The five texts studied here demonstrate how such deconstruction takes place, in the Israeli context, through the contrived use of *simulation*. My argument is that the reprocessing of myths through and into simulations provides a powerful medium of social appropriation. Through simulation, dismantled collective memories can be disenfranchised from the realm of elitist hegemony. In this manner, myths are detached from their origins and inserted into the cultural flow of everyday consumption. The simulation provides an easily manipulated cultural form, divorced from personal commitment or collective ideologies (Baudrillard 1988). In other words, while the simulations we are about to encounter are all ideological and to some extent subversive, they are not self-declared ideologies. Simulations elude the scholarly program of which myths are an important part. Their authority structure is much less explicit and visible, and much more diffused and covert. In that respect they match the invisible authority structure of late modernity (Bauman 1992).

I use the term "simulation" to denote a social text that is a staged production of self-display where the "self" is undergoing transformation. A simulation therefore combines several elements: it is public, it is dramatic, and it plays with meanings. In this definition I am somewhat extending Baudrillard's concept of the "simulacrum" as a copy that has no original—a reflection that once represented reality and, while taking off from that reality, has become independent and now replaces reality (1983, 1988). Baudrillard's diagnosis was later developed by postmodernist theorists who view contemporary society as largely cinematic, a "voyeuristic society" where the cinema, the TV and the commercial are our reality (Denzin 1992; Jameson 1991).

When speaking of simulations, I am borrowing Baudrillard's term and extending it to denote texts that play with representation. While myths are always solemn and grave, simulations are often playful. To be engaged in a simulation is to observe something that represents "reality" in a reflexive, knowingly distorted manner. Simulations often toy with reality and its myths. The simulation is often a wink of reflexivity; an acknowledgement that reality is too complicated and myths are too simplistic. In other words, the simulation represents the "fringes" of myth—and therefore often becomes the myth of society's fringes.

The five chapters illustrate five simulations. In chapter 1, which deals with the Sephardi neighborhood, I describe the staged production of a "community," contrived by its Sephardi residents in order to cleanse the neighborhood of its ethnic stigma. In chapter 2, which deals with Holocaust delegations, I examine the simulation of the "Holocaust" during school preparations. The handbooks used by different schools for the preparation of students are examined as a window to the contested terrain where certain aspects of the "Holocaust" are to be commemorated, while others are doomed to be forgotten. Chapter 3 looks at "This Is It in the Gulf" ("This Is It"), a satirical TV series staged during the Gulf War, as a serialized simulation of a new collectivism in the context of a war that triggered feelings of national impotence rather than the usual script of soldiering. In chapter 4, the dispirited (simulated) rebellion of Israeli youth is examined through a popular Tel-Avivian group film called *Late Summer Blues*. The last chapter examines the media-screened commemoration that followed Rabin's assassination as a simulation of "we-feeling," a national grief staged in particular sites of memory and by youth that claimed a stake in collective memory.

The five chapters can also be looked at as an *ascending* order of simulations. We start with a deprived community. This is a concrete, geographically bound place that traditionally calls for a realistic ethnography. However, even this seemingly traditional zone of ethno-graphic realism has its simulations. These surface in special occasions such as rituals and festivals, which the first chapter describes in detail. The second chapter focuses on textual representations of the Holocaust in the handbooks of youth tours and delegations. The third and fourth chapters deal with media representations (TV and film). The fifth and last chapter focuses on the staged reactions to Rabin's death, describing them as a "carnival." While all chapters deal with simulations, each chapter starts with a different reference point, moving from the con-crete to the abstract. Each chapter hence provides its own account of the literal and metaphorical ties between Israeli youth and the Zionist myths/simulations.

Youth and Post-Zionist Simulations

Youth features in the chapters in various ways. In the case of the deprived community, it was the neighborhood youth that played a major role in the enactment of community. The local youth performed in front of the audience in the community festival—a festival described in chapter 1 as the peak and culmination of symbolic community. In the case of Holocaust delegations, youth—the delegation participants from various schools—is the subject of competing nationalistic ideolo-gies. As for the two examples of popular media that I discuss, *Late Sum-mer Blues* is a youth film, while "This Is It" is a TV program aimed at youth. Finally, the last chapter on Rabin's commemoration recounts the extraordinary story of the "candle kids," youth who voluntarily gath-ered to mourn and commemorate Rabin.

Locating youth as the target audience—and main agent—of simu-lation is perhaps neither a coincidence nor a surprise. The staged pro-ductions with which Israeli youth experiment in this book—TV, film, performance, delegations, commemoration—are a symbol of leisure. All these activities are not part of real life but reflections of it: a TV program that reflects the Gulf War, a film commenting on growing up in Tel-Aviv, educational handbooks that frame the Holocaust, redemption festivals and commemoration rites. These are all happenings that, while representing media and modes of articulation that adult society regards as "light" and "leisurely," actually deal with serious matters at the heart of Israeli identity. They deal with the core myths of Israeli society, but in a playful, leisurely way—a way suitable and acceptable for youth.

As playful experiments with serious issues, these simulations follow the postmodern emphasis on secular ritual (Turner 1969,1977). Modernism has appropriated the myth from the hands of religion, and created a mythology of nationalism (in the Israeli context, see for example the modern national myths of the Fall of Masada or the Battle of Tel-Hai). Postmodern society has gone beyond the modernist appropriation of myths, de-constructing nationalism and questioning its borders and narratives. Pilgrimages are currently made to Disneyland (or the local mall) rather than, or in addition to, the Vatican, Mecca or Jerusalem.

Traditionally, myths were sacred, communal experiences involving public worship in designated sites, and leading to an unreserved commitment to the collectivity. The simulations discussed here restage such myths in the realm of popular culture. The experience of participation is more individualistic and reflexive; the mythical object is the TV or the silver screen; and the resultant commitment is reserved and often sectorial.

It is interesting to look at the shift from myths to simulations, as reflected by Israeli youth, in both a structural and historical context. As a result of their social moratorium—being betwixt and between childhood and adulthood—youth experiences a double bind. Youth is expected to comply with mid-life rules while being given leeway to criticize these rules. In Israel, a society that recently experienced a shift from collectivism to individualism, the shift of Israeli youth should also be located in a historical context. Generally speaking, the Zionist ethos was carried by youth—first the *Haluzim* (pioneers), then the *Sabras* (native-born Israeli). Zionism celebrated the youthful ethos of cultivating a new body (Max Nordau's 'Judaism with muscles') through cultivating the land and the 'conquering of labor.' These romantic ideas were born in the intellectual milieu of nineteenth century European nationalism, and Zionist youth was to a large extent fashioned after similar German and Austro-Hungarian youth movements. In other words, the identity of youth has always been to some

7

extent a reflection of external processes, in early Zionism as well as in post-Zionist Israel.

Early Zionism, in the heyday of nation-building, was a rite of passage in its own right (or at least is now seen as such). This meant that social commitment was much stronger and often demanded the sacrifice of one's familiar surroundings, family ties and even individualism. Youth was at the front of all that: the pioneers (often youngsters in their early 20s) saw themselves as soldiers in a battle for a territory (Palestine), a nation (Ivrim), and a language (Hebrew); on these three 'sacred treasures' of Zionist youth, see Elboym-Dror 1996; Shapira 1990. Gradually, Zionism has institutionalized various patterns of youth socialization that were inscribed with the values of collectivism and the ethos of 'collective contribution' (see also Rapoport and Lomsky-Feder 1988). Such documented patterns of youth socialization include, for example, compulsory military conscription at age 18 (Lieblich 1995; Levy, Bleich and Chen 1987), the youth movement (Katriel 1987; Shapira and Peleg 1984), the national service of religious-Zionist female adolescents (Rapoport, Penso and Garb 1994), community service prior to military enlistment (Avrahami and Dar 1993), and even name books at school (Herzog and Shapira 1986).

The autonomy of youth as a cultural space has been recently augmented by global processes of consumerism: TV, fashion, music, MTV, video, the internet, and so on. Youth is the prime carrier of globalization. Youngsters are the new breed of global consumers, living in a virtual time where the same music/film/TV star is worshiped around the world and where youth fashions transgress national, geographical, and gender boundaries. The postmodern compression of time-space is perhaps nowhere more apparent than in the everyday lives of teenagers.

In Baudrillard's view, the simulation spells a departure from the realist text of rationalization, nation-building and other modernization projects. Locating these simulations in the Israeli context therefore also positions Israel in the global context of the flow of culture, since many of these simulations and their mediating channels—TV, cinema, documentaries, and so on—hinge on Western, mainly American, cultural impact. Sociologists and anthropologists of Israel have traditionally followed the accepted wisdom of their profession and regarded their turf (Israeli society) as a close unit—a single source of reasons for its own national logic. This professional tendency has produced "regional studies" around the world with an emphasis on exceptionalism (Friedman 1994). This book sets out to examine Israel not merely on the terms of its "uniqueness" but also as a place influenced by global processes. From a perspective of political economy, similar premises are employed in the colonialist model (see Shafir 1989). However, this study focuses on cultural, rather than economic, processes, and does so from a post-colonial perspective.

I therefore locate Israeli culture not in Wallerstein's (1974) world-system but in Hannerz's (1989) "global ecumene" where global cultural forms—such as television, cinema, music and youth culture in general—find their various forms of localization, domestication, pidginization and hybridization. The popularity, in Israel, of these global media forms, has brought with it the advent of the simulation as an accountable and pervasive means of social representation. As Burgin (1996: 266) argues, with the flow of culture from "the imperial Western metropolis to its colonized 'peripheries,' the very possibility of the distinction between margins and center is eroded...as each 'we' spins its own yarn of origin." This book is about the story of origin that various groups are currently spinning in Israel. It opens with the tale of origin told by the elderly women group, but its main textual corpus deals with representations of youth culture. Simulations have become, particularly for youth, a popular avenue for social representation, identity searches and inter-generational conflicts precisely because of their lack of commitment and playful flow. In late capitalism, following the flow of popular culture, simulations have become populist and playful whereas myths are considered—perhaps paradoxically—both elitist and radical. This is indeed the local case with the Zionist myth, that has been traditionally carried by the elitist and secular Labor Party, but has been gradually appropriated by nationalist-religious groups.

Forget Zionism?

The five simulations studied in this book illustrate a polyphony whose multiple voices interpret the once single Zionist myth. A concise description of this myth should thus serve as the necessary background for the following analysis. I do not intend to provide a step-by-step analysis of the historical changes of Zionist narratives. Rather, I focus on contemporary texts, in which the change (or debunking) of narratives is accelerated and their contours are reflected and illuminated. To say that Israeli society is undergoing a process of myth debunking is not new in itself. As Wistrich and Ohana recently claimed,

The heroic view of the Israeli War of Independence as a struggle of the few against the many or of a uniquely peace-loving Zionist movement facing intransigently hostile Arab enemies has been challenged by a new generation of Israeli historians…. Along with the war of 1948 (and virtually all of Israel's subsequent wars), the heroes of Zionism and Israel have also come in for a battering…. The old heroes, the ideal of self-sacrificing patriotism, collectivist ideologies or the naive cult of the Sabra (native-born Israeli) seem increasingly out of date (1995: vi).

This may be true for revisionist historians in academic circles, leftist and liberal intelligentsia, or the new high-tech professionals seeking access to the global economy. However, these trends do not constitute the main bulk of Israeli cultural practices. The trendy debunking of national myths has recently had its counter-reaction in the form of the rise to power of the right-wing Likud Party, as well as the ethnically fueled religious parties (notably SHAS [Sephardic Guardians of the Torah]), in the last elections. It was the Likud government headed by Prime Minister Benjamin Netanyahu that had halted the peace process, whose motion was perceived as threatening the fundamental truths of Israeli nationality. These truths, which center on power, common blood, and territory, belong to the realm of the Zionist myth, whose legacy is outlined in the following section.

Capturing Time-Space

There is a paradox inherent in our thinking about time. On the one hand, we employ a pragmatic assumption regarding the "arrow of time." We believe that time is a one-way, progressive, and irreversible phenomenon. On the other hand, we believe that—ideally—the future should be based on the past. Myths represent one way of arresting the flow of time and hence of reconciling these contradictory assertions. Myths happen in a time which is always and everywhere—an "eternal now." It is "dreamtime" or perhaps not a time but rather a cultural *space*. Most myths are narratives that anchor the present in the past (Cohen 1973; Eliade 1965, 1969).

This is virtually what Zionism is all about. The ingathering of the exiled, the building of Zion, the creation of a new Hebrew person— these were visions of both mythical breadth and historical focus. Zionism was constructed as a myth of genesis—a national redemption much along the romantic lines of nineteenth century European national movements—in order to "put the Jews back in history." The timeless Jewish yearning from around its exiled scattering was harnessed to a specific time-space—the land of Israel in the twentieth century. The focus on national power, unity, and pioneering as advocated in the "melting pot" doctrine of Ben-Gurion's statism (*mamlakhtiut*) was therefore a direct continuation of the Zionist, pre-state ethos. There is no doubt that these narratives were a functional necessity for a country poor in natural resources and caught up in an ongoing military conflict, a country that depended on motivation and collective determination. However, these narratives also paved the way for a system of normative control, coercion, and subjugation.

The Israeli discourse of collectivism oscillates between history and territory, attempting to "recapture" history, re-create national life, in the new/old Hebraic homeland, the land of Israel. The master commemorative narrative that was used to reconnect "old" history (such as the Second Commonwealth) and contemporary Zionist time while doing away with two thousand years of exile is described by Zerubavel (1995), who traced this process through three major narratives: the Battle of Tel-Hai, the Bar-Kokhba Revolt, and the Fall of Masada.

The Zionist periodization of Jewish history is based on the primacy of the people-land bond. The past is divided into antiquity and exile. Contemporary national revival is associated with the "golden age" of the ancient, autonomous, Hebrew-speaking and proud Jews that are rooted in their land. At the same time, it is also dissociated from the negative image of the exile, that comes to be regarded as the uprooting of the Jews from their land. The Holocaust had a major role in crystallizing the negative image of the diaspora Jew as "lamb to the slaughter"; it is only recently that Israelis have reconsidered the meaning of the Holocaust, for example through the popular educational practice of youth delegations. An additional myth that has come to bridge the gap between antiquity and national redemption is the plot structure of the "few against many," for example. Historians of Israeli collective memory, who set out to map that process, located it in the narratives of nation-building in the pre-state Jewish community in Palestine. Sociologists such as Zerubavel (1995), Katriel (1989) and Ben-Yehuda (1995), who described such collective scripts for national mobilization, are largely uncritical of their reception as well as their dark and coercive aspects. Moreover, sociologists have largely ignored the major problem of the Zionist ethos in contemporary Israeli society, often because the "contemporary" is pushed beyond the discussion.

The problem currently experienced by Israelis is that of deciding between the mythical time of the Zionist ethos, the time of "for the land and the lord," versus the historical time of "normalization," signified by the peace process, the evacuation of occupied territories, and globalization. In other words, Israelis face the problem of having to adapt the territorial Zionist ethos into a post-Zionist ideology which will be less territorial and more timely. It is a burning problem of continuity and change. The master narrative and its alternatives—the egg and its disguises—are further illustrated in the following section through the images of the body and the territory.

Myths of the Body and the Territory

My rhetorical use of "myths," "dreams," and "narratives" is intended to set the scene for an alternative reading of texts that have long shaped the Israeli mind. Even though these narratives have recently come under scrutiny, the majority of Israeli sociologists have dealt with "collective memory" in a manner that reproduces its functional hegemony through describing (rather than deconstructing) its "master" commemorative narratives. Like many "mainstream" sociological analyses, these studies of collective memory have often ignored the body as a locus of representation, directing their sociological attention to more abstract fields. Yet the nexus between territory and body has been one of the major constructs of Zionist ideology.[1]

Israeli culture has been involved with the construction of bodies as part of the ongoing shaping of its own collective identity. Israel's continuing involvement in an armed conflict with its Arab neighbors has created a society deeply concerned with territorial borders as well as body boundaries. Social tropes such as the pioneer, the *Sabra*, and the soldier, symbolized the submersion of the private and the personal within the body politic. The importance of the pioneer was derived, among other factors, from its involvement in settling the land. Settling was a central pioneering activity that meant, literally, rerooting in the land. As Ben-Ari and Bilu (1997:4) state, "acts of settlement (such as those of 'Tower and Stockade'), and the rhetoric of place attending them, have been at the heart of Israel's nation-building ethos."

The *Sabra* was, similarly, the carrier of the collectivity's aspirations of expansion in time (generativity) and space (territory). The mandatory military service became a social-evaluative network for *Sabras* and an acculturation platform for new immigrants. The pioneer and the *Sabra* were both carnal, as well as metaphysical, constructions. They were bodies in the service of the nation, rerooted in their territory, providing a remedy for the national degeneration of the "rootless" diaspora Jew.[2] They were the inhabitants of a novel and mystified Israeli landscape, the products of an elaborate system of socialization, including school syllabi, nature hikes as "spiritual journeys," agricultural festivals, archeological excavations, settlement museums, monuments and other geographical sites for civil pilgrimage (see the collection of essays in Ben-Ari and Bilu [1997], as well as Almog [1994]).

The *Sabra*-fighter—the conqueror and settler of land—became the authentic representative of the native-born Israeli. His (and more often her) image was also sold abroad in order to promote the Zionist project among world Jewry. The act of promotion is (unreflectively) documented in books such as *The First Million Sabras* (Russcol and Banai 1970) and *Women of Israel* (Waagenaar 1961). These books celebrate collective traits and reify the concept of a national mentality. This is often done through generalizations that contrapose the "new Sabras" with their Jewish ancestors, the power of the body with the 'people of the book.' According to Russcol and Banai,

> The Sabra is generally a head taller than his father, often blonde and freckled, often blue-eyed and snub-nosed. He is cocky, robustly built, and likes to walk in open sandals in a free-swinging, lazy slouch. He speaks Hebrew in a rapid fire sputter.... In a sense, he is a Hebrew-speaking WASP. (1970:4)

Waagenaar (1960:5) similarly advertises the "Israeli woman" as the first thing that strikes a visitor to Israel—"her erect walk, the absence of make-up, the fact that so many of them are pregnant." The image that was successfully sold abroad became a local discourse of exceptionalism. In Hebrew literature a similar biological alteration is described and connected to a life of labor in Israel's tough climate. The *Sabra* as the "startling mutation of the desert" (Russcol and Banai 1970:5) is often described as "free of uniforms, one of the *Jama'a* (Arabic for "the gang"), with short khaki pants, his blouse open to the belt, tanned face.... In short: one of us" (from a *palmach* booklet cited in Ben-Eliezer 1995:121; see also Maoz 1988).

Such body symbolism was augmented in an immigrant society that lacked one uniting cultural framework for symbolic communication. The body became visible in almost all of the myths of national redemption: the glorification of youth, militarism, fertility, birth, and death (particularly in battle). The view of the individual as the carrier of collective ideals and as subordinate to them was a common thread characterizing the otherwise antagonistic camps of the left-wing pioneers and the right-wing nationalists. The cultural space of Zionism was a territory populated by bodies of workers, soldiers, and brave wives and mothers.

Israeli Collectivism in Retrospective

As a discourse of signification and control, collectivism presents itself as taken-for-granted, beyond refute and criticism. From Zionist thinkers to Israeli citizens, collectivism has been long perceived not as threatening the autonomy of the individual but rather as an emancipatory force. Collectivism became the "civil religion" of Israel, the larger frame of reference through which other issues and "problems"—such as militarization, the "melting pot" of immigration, the relations with the diaspora and with the Palestinians—were all defined and accounted for. Collectivism is still a binding force that recaptures the public sphere in times of national distress, such as war and terrorism.

The Israeli collectivity was recently rediscovered by Israeli sociologists. This rediscovery, publicly manifested in a plethora of scholarly books, conferences and debates, has emerged along three distinct lines. The first line takes a critical and theoretical form of reflecting on the discourse of Israeli sociology. It seeks to unveil the ideological premises that fashioned the way in which sociology has been implemented in Israel, and the ideologically colored lenses this sociology has provided for magnifying, problematizing as well as neglecting various social issues. The second line of inquiry, ethnographic and descriptive in nature, does not question the worldview of sociology. Rather, it works within its framework, setting out to illuminate the centrality of collective scripts. The third approach combines critical theory with "subaltern history," offering alternative readings of central historical events in the formation of the Israeli nation-state—most notably the 1948 War (see Kimmerling 1992:447; Morris 1988, 1990; Pappe 1992). The opening up of the history of the 1948 War of Independence could mean the birth of a "new historiography" (Pappe 1988, 1993), different from the "nationalized versions" of positivist, or "pedestrian" (Kedourie 1984) histories.[3] The same, of course, could be said in regard to another turning point in Israeli history: the Six-Day War (1967) (see Kimmerling 1992: 447).

Israeli political sociology, claim its critics, has been recently undergoing a belated crisis of reflexivity, a crisis generated by social and political changes which seem to overwhelm Israeli society at large. "Since 1967, the year of the occupation of Arab territories," writes Ram (1989:255), "and more pointedly after 1977, the year the Labor Party fell and the right-wing Likud gained power, events themselves have exposed the inadequacies of the paradigm that has dominated Israeli sociological thought for about three decades." This critical stance is also shared by Kimmerling (1992:446), who argues that "explicit and implicit cultural commitments, perceived existential needs, and class, ethnic and national interests, have shaped the way Israeli sociologists portray the basic features of Israeli society." One of the most prominent pieces of evidence to this biased sociological worldview is the absence of the social issue of Arabs in Israel. Coming from another theoretical perspective, Smooha (1992:2) argues that "researchers tend to conceive of Arab-Jewish relations in terms of Jewish intransigence or Arab radicalization."

The conflict between the Jewish collectivity and its significant other—the Arabs—resulted in the placement of the two on opposite time lines. Israelis were placed on a progressive, scientific, historical time line. Arabs, on the contrary, were relegated to the realm of primitive society and placed on a mythical, timeless, and cyclical course. These opposite time lines were used to construct two imaginary territories—ours and theirs.

The "Orientalism" of Israeli Arabists has recently been challenged by an upsurge of social science research which is, in the words of Rabinowitz (1997:18), "considerably less committed to the Zionist agenda or altogether dismissive of it." Rabinowitz's own "ethnography of exclusion in the Galilee," aptly entitled *Overlooking Nazareth*, is the most recent example of this trend, joining a growing list of young Israeli researchers such as Shalev (1992), Pappe (1988), Regev (1993), Morris (1994), Shlaim (1990) and Peled (1992), as well as a new generation of Palestinian researchers (Sa'adi 1992).

In contrast to the long-established invisibility of Palestinians and Israeli-Arabs, the Sepharadim (Jews of North African and Arab origin) were "over-visible" for Israeli applied anthropologists. Since the 1960s, many Israeli anthropologists were employed by the Jewish Agency to research immigrant settlements and immigrants' "acculturation." As a research tradition, it entailed the use of a functionalist and developmental framework for understanding cultural change. This mode of representation is arguably still prominent among many Israeli anthropologists today. This view served as justification for decades of harsh immigration "absorption policies."[4] An ample amount of research examples is cited in both Ram (1989) and Kimmerling (1992), and I will not detail them here. Generally speaking, these demonstrate how the collective ideology of nation-building, of which Israeli socio-anthropology was—and to a large extent still is—part and parcel (Van-Toeffelen 1978), has reproduced itself by generating pre-assumptions regarding the boundaries of the unit under consideration, the terminology used, the problems posed, and the topics deemed appropriate for research. Epistemological frameworks are thus turned into the taken-for-granted ontological contours of social reality.

Beyond Collectivism

The wars of 1967 and 1973 initiated a process of change in the dominant myths, that eventually led to their open debunking in the 1990s. The 1967 War spawned the occupied territories; the 1973 War, a crisis of confidence in the military. In 1977, the rise in influence of "Second Israel," composed of underprivileged Sepharadim, brought the Likud to power for the first time. The descent of militarism, one of the cornerstones of Israeli collectivism, joined after 1973 with the rise of capitalist free market and the election economics employed by the Likud government since 1977. The abundance of new commodities and the rise in living conditions further took Israeli society into its new phase of individualism. Former consensus and univocal elite dominance were replaced by conflicts (regarding the occupied territories and the peace process) and a plurality of political power bases.

There is now a feeling, quite common among Israelis, that collectivism was part of their youth (and of youth generally), while individualism—accompanied by "cynicism and fatigue"—is a kind of mid-life crisis. "Israel," wrote Elon already twenty-five years ago (1971:322), "resembles a man racing ahead with his eyes turned back." The eyes are turned back, but what they see is the "master commemorative narrative" of the Ashkenazi establishment. The collective gaze still prescribes, to a large extent, the ways in which Israelis remember their past.

The five chapters of this book, five dreams and their simulations, all seek to undo these invisible bonds that have harnessed the popular

Israeli imagination to its collective master narrative. Throughout, I adopt the view currently addressed by various proponents of "dialogical" anthropology. This view emphasizes the sharing of ethnographic authority with the voices of informants.[5] This call is becoming ever more urgent as "the former subjects or objects of study are not only becoming an audience, and a critical one at that, but they are becoming anthropologists themselves" (Caplan 1988:17). Let us therefore lend an ear to the following voices, and find there both the master narrative and its marginal notes.

NOTES

1. The linkage between body and territory was discussed by Mary Douglas (1966, 1973, 1997), who focused on the Jews as a particular example. Douglas created a distinct genre of inquiry into the role of body metaphors, especially in conjunction with social processes that are risky or dangerous. One of her major arguments (1973)—that a society deeply concerned with external borders is also deeply concerned with body boundaries—provides a connection between Jewish and Israeli embodiment.

2. For further sociological discussion of the pioneer and Sabra (see Almog 1994; Ben-Eliezer 1995; Katriel 1987; Rubinstein 1977).

3. For recent sociological interventions in the collectivist worldview of Israeli society from the perspective of the Palestinians and Israeli-Arabs (see Bashara 1992; Beit-Halachmi 1992; Kimmerling 1992; Kimmerling and Migdal 1992; Morris 1990; Peled 1992; Smooha 1990).

4 See a recent discussion of this debate in Shokeid (1992); for a critique of the failure of reflexivity in most Israeli anthropology see also Kunda (1992) and also Gurevitch and Aran (1991). On a more general level, since the last decade there has been a steady accumulation of critical literature discussing anthropology and the colonial encounter or the politics of ethnography in "developing" societies: see Escobar (1991); Apffel-Marglin and Marglin (1990); Asad (1973); Bennet and Bowen (1988); Clifford and Marcus (1986).

5. See Clifford (1983, 1986); Kirschner (1987); Sanjek (1990); and the special 1990 issue of The Journal of Contemporary Ethnography, dedicated to ethnographic research writing.

1. RESOLVING SOCIAL INEQUALITIES
The Ethnic Discourse

⋐∞⋑

*T*he focus of this chapter is a deprived neighborhood in central Israel. During the time of my research there, this place was a typical low-status, inner-city neighborhood mostly inhabited by Sepharadim—Jewish immigrants from Asia and North Africa (about 63 percent of all residents). The neighborhood was a demonstration of the ethnic cleavage in Israel between Sepharadim and Ashkenazim (Jews of European and American origin). This cleavage is still very much present in contemporary Israel. The 1996 figures of the Central Bureau of Statistics, for example, show that poor neighborhoods are still home mainly to Sepharadim, who suffer most from unemployment (12 percent on average, in contrast to 3 percent in Tel-Aviv). The ethnic fissure dates back to the 1950s and 1960s, when immigrants from places like Morocco, Iraq, Egypt, Yemen, and Syria met with an Ashkenazi establishment, bent on forging a Western, secular culture. From the mid-1950s on, new arrivals were often dispersed to far-flung "development" towns. The dispersion created a dual topographical structure, divided between a "First Israel" in the Ashkenazi, urban core and a "Second Israel" in the Sephardi, rural peripheries. Second Israel was growing in alienation, which burst forth in protests in the 1950s and 1970s.

A host of social indicators shows that many of the gaps between first-generation Ashkenazim and Sepharadim persist, or have grown worse, in the second generation. Sepharadim make up roughly half of the Jewish population, but only one-fourth of university students. The vast majority of prison inmates are Sepharadim. Forty-eight percent of the white-collar workers are Ashkenazi, while 54 percent of the blue-collar workforce are Sepharadim. The average Ashkenazi income is one-and-a-half times the average Sephardi income.

While Israeli sociologists have all admitted to the existence of ethnic inequalities, they did so from different viewpoints. Ben-Zadok (1993) usefully identifies four such viewpoints: functional, pluralist, elite and dependency. The functional approach (e.g., Horowitz and Lissak 1978) views ethnicity as a temporary state that coexists with value consensus. A related approach, usually termed as pluralist, views ethnicity as the basis for a constantly changing power distribution with no value consensus, but with compromises and cooperation (e.g., Smooha 1978; Yishai 1987). Proponents of both the elite (e.g., Shapiro 1978) and dependency (e.g., Swirski 1981) approaches blame Israeli scholars for their unwillingness to criticize the egalitarian and pluralist assumptions of their own society. Both of these alternative approaches—elite and dependency—emphasize stratification and conflict, the former (elite) in the context of the politics of the center, and the latter (dependency) in the ethnic division of labor to which Sepharadim are subjected.

The ethnic cleavage has spawned many attempts for bridging the gap, central among them being "project renewal" (hereafter "the Project"). The concept of "renewal neighborhoods" became part of Israeli social life after the initiation of the Program for Rehabilitation and Renewal of Neighborhoods in Israel in 1977 by the government of Menachem Begin (see Carmon and Hill 1984, and the International Committee on Project Renewal Evaluation ["Project Renewal" or "the Project"], 1981). Since 1977, ninety neighborhoods in Israel have become part of this nation-wide rehabilitation project. What follows is an ethnography of one such renewal neighborhood, beginning with the "hard facts" that determine the day-to-day conditions of existence of the residents, and proceeding to the world of images and metaphors which residents "live by" (for an elaborated discussion of that neighborhood, see Hazan 1990).

The neighborhood in which the research was conducted—which I shall call Arod—is part of a city situated in the center of the country, and has a population of about six thousand. It is located on the outskirts of the town and is separated from most of its other residential areas by open land. In the years 1981 to 1986, the average size of households in the neighborhood was 3.7 and the population was relatively young: 36 percent of the residents are aged 14 or under, while those aged 65 and above comprise 8.8 percent. The rate of families with four or more children (up to age 17) among all families with children was 23 percent (compared to 12 percent among the Jewish population of Israel). The neighborhood's residents were and still are characterized by extremely heterogeneous ethnic origin, stemming from some 32 countries, mostly from Asia and North Africa (some 63 percent of all residents are Sepharadim). Approximately 14 percent were Israeli-born and 22 percent (the Ashkenazim) were born in Europe (mainly eastern Europe) and America. The rate of those with partial or complete elementary education among the 15 to 44 age-group in the neighborhood was 30 percent, and the rate of non-employed was above the national average: 48.7 percent among men and 72 percent among women (the respective rates in the general population were then 32.9 percent and 55.8 percent). The level of family income was also relatively low, standing at 34 percent below the national average (for further comparative data, see Ofek 1993).

The range of employment and housing opportunities available to most of the residents was limited, and they were well aware of this. Moreover, an improvement in living conditions may have been gained either by a move to less expensive areas, such as a development town or a community settlement on the West Bank, or to a different part of the neighborhood itself. For most of them, any thought of moving to the central area of the large city that lay in enticing proximity was an unrealistic (although captivating) dream. Nevertheless, many of the residents reported a feeling of belonging to the place in the sense of its being a human environment rather than an area of residence. A taxi driver expressed this sentiment in the following typical manner: "I'll do my best to leave this neighborhood, but my heart will remain here forever." The main expectations of Project Renewal were that an improved quality of life and a more agreeable physical environment would be expressed in a commensurate rise in the prices of apartments, the sale of which would enable a move to a different area. Identification with the neighborhood, such as it was, took the form of dependence on a local social network, the importance of which is evident among a population that struggles to fulfill its material, employment and educational expectations on its own. This mutual support was not attributed to the neighborhood's existence as a socio-territorial entity. On the contrary, residents felt that "in spite of this screwed-up neighborhood, the people here are nice."

A paradoxical need thus arose to abolish the neighborhood while maintaining it for the options it provided for social security. Residents spoke with revulsion about various aspects common in the neighborhood, such as drug abuse and crime, and went as far as to condemn the place as a neighborhood without a future. Many of these same residents, however, referred with affection to what they termed "the neighborhood spirit." The dilemma confronting residents was whether and how to rid themselves of the neighborhood while conserving its "spirit." In order to achieve this feat, one of the major strategies employed was rhetoric.

Project Renewal had a decisive role in imparting, justifying and disseminating this language, which I broadly refer to as "the language of community." Residents learned that in order to communicate usefully with project officials they would be advised to adapt their speech to the argot of the organization that concentrated such vast resources. The ability to negotiate a share in the distribution of resources, such as housing allowances, establishment of various clubs in the vicinity of their homes, positions on the Project's staff, etc., was largely determined by the residents' contacts with local centers of power. These centers—local committees, officeholders owing their livelihood to the Project, and various community services—were all part of the Project's organizational structure, and thus partook in an ongoing organizational discourse whose declared purpose was to turn the neighborhood into a community. This discourse took place in many meetings at which interests were presented, debates held and decisions made, as well as in the course of daily chats and contacts among providers of services, and between them and residents. This discourse, which originated in a bureaucratic argot foreign to the local residents and typical of Project Renewal in general, facilitated communication in four spheres: among project officials; with residents; with the authorities and institutions to which the local project was linked and which served as its basis; and with the "adopting" community in the United States.

The communicative power of the Project's language thus acquired a local dominance that relied on ideological hegemony, according to which the Project's objective was to enable the local community to merge with (or become acculturated to) "mainstream" Israeli society while abolishing the neighborhood's (and residents') original identity/stigma. I try to outline the rough contours of this discourse by describing five of its "root metaphors," which—I argue—are also the key images in the general discourse of ethnicity in contemporary Israel.

22

Five Root Metaphors

Residents

These are perceived as a generalized entity, not necessarily identified with place of residence. The "residents" are not equivalent to the neighborhood, and may thus be separated from it. This is a dynamic entity that possesses a dual transformative potential. It may join up with those "unhealthy" elements found in the neighborhood, or sever its connections with the neighborhood and reach the level of "ordinary Israeli citizens, as in Ra'anana, Kiron or Tel-Aviv," in the words of one of the project activists. The "positive" potential was supposedly to be encouraged by adopting certain life styles, with particular emphasis on complementary education, that characterize well-established localities. Thus, computer courses, various educational clubs and sports activities flourished in the neighborhood. All these were supposed to comprise a cultural mechanism whereby the symbolic entity called "residents" was to elevate itself from the stigma of its neighborhood. Alongside this mechanism functioned a political mechanism termed "resident participation," which was designed to allocate a role to neighborhood residents in the decision-making process with regard to priorities and distribution of resources concerning the planning of their lives in their place of residence.

This "resident participation," which supposedly occurred on several decision-making levels, from steering committees to implementation of the programs in the field, was the object of severe criticism and even open ridicule and expressions of skepticism as to its sincerity. As one of the residents put it: "In Herzlia there is no 'resident participation' because there the residents participate anyway. Only here is this fig leaf necessary, so that they can do what they like, supposedly with our consent." "They" are the establishment's representatives, who include the Project's salaried officials—both locals and those from the outside—and other office holders involved in decision making at the local level. But "they" also refers to Israeli society, since serious questions about their sense of belonging to it constituted one of Arod's residents' central dilemmas.

Israeli Society

An ambivalent image signifying belonging and identification on the one hand, and a sense of rejection and detachment on the other. The tension between these two poles was generally apparent when "Israeli society" was mentioned; while national symbols such as the army and even "good old Israeli songs" engendered enthusiastic identification among residents, much frustration was caused by the labeling of their neighborhood as a deprived area. The neighborhood's very inclusion in Project Renewal, in itself considered an achievement to which many deprived areas aspired, exacerbated the sense of detachment and alienation from Israeli society. When the local project was praised for its achievements, one of the residents reacted by quoting a Hebrew proverb: "We were head of the foxes, not even a tail to the lions." Both the residents in general and those active in the Project were well aware that full integration into what they conceived as "Israeli society" could take place only at the expense of denouncing the neighborhood's identity. The attitude toward the country's political regime reflected this ambivalence. The then prime minister, Menachem Begin, who had been among the initiators of the national project, enjoyed widespread admiration, expressed in terms such as: "Begin is our father, we owe him everything." Several ministers in Begin's government, however, who were involved in Project Renewal, were at times roundly criticized, as were their minions—directors of ministries and their officials. The residents' attitude toward the army was stamped with the same duality. Admiration of military symbols was shared by most residents. This was apparent in the adoption by the local youth movement of a military-style uniform, and in the manner in which visiting army officers were feted. But the fact that some of the local youngsters were not drafted into the army on grounds of social incompatibility was a sore point, about which people were embarrassed and complained. Rehabilitation programs operated by the army, in which several of the neighborhood's youngsters were included, served only to exacerbate the feeling of rejection within the general sense of identification with the national collectivity. A television documentary portraying the arduous and tortuous process of an Arod youngster's acceptance to an army unit was conceived by residents as a mark of Cain on the neighborhood's forehead. One of them put it this way: "Now the entire country knows who we are, and all who see us shall know us" (an explicit allusion to the biblical mark of Cain).

Whereas the Project set itself up as leverage to ease the process of integration into "Israeli society," its very existence paradoxically loaded even weightier stigmas than before onto the neighborhood's image. Any activity regarded as evidence of the Project's success also emphasized the neighborhood's degradation and marginality, which had necessitated the activity in the first place.

Community

According to the neighborhood's residents, this concept was not in daily usage before the Project entered their lives. The term became one of the national Project's main semantic apparatuses, since it was extremely useful in creating a smooth rhetoric in all spheres of the Project, thereby helping to blur the conflicts inherent in them. Its qualities of symbolic opaqueness and social cleanliness rendered the term acceptable and innocuous.[1] In this respect "community" is an undefined social unit, that is neither a "neighborhood," nor a "development area," nor a "special attention area," nor a "deprived neighborhood." It signifies a framework that transforms all these into a desirable way of life without any negative connotations, suited to the modern, Western world to which it aspires. This Western world was represented in the Project not only as an ideal model comprising quality of life, technological sophistication, comfortable housing and attractive surroundings, but also as a concrete entity manifested by the adopting sister-city communities from the diaspora.[2] These were regarded not only as a bountiful source of funds that would help the neighborhood to develop into a "community," but also as a model to be emulated, and to which the neighborhood was now linked by a strong, continuous bond, expressed in reciprocal visits, hospitality and joint planning of services and facilities, which had replaced the "haphazard and casual connection of the past." The concept was freely bandied about at every opportunity. It was easier to talk of "communities" rather than of "neighborhoods," since the expression did not require territorial definition or accuracy, was free of unpleasant connotations, and enabled the establishment of a rhetorical relationship of equality between adopter and adopted, purveyors of services and their clients, residents and establishment figures. It replaced existing images with new ones, and belonged to the language of "renewal" and "wellbeing," rather than the language of "development" and "welfare."

However, the most important characteristic was probably the nucleus common to every settlement or group of people seeking a future with a quality of life independent of any previous economic, social or cultural background. The proliferation of "community settlements" during this period, and the attendant media campaign encouraging the young, energetic and ambitious to join them, added a taste of belonging to a different Israeli society, one that was able to shed the impediments of past divisions. The aspiration to become a "community" was presented by the project workers in Arod as a vision of a different social future, which the neighborhood's residents would be able to realize only if they were to change beyond recognition. The binding quality of the concept of "community" facilitated rhetorical patching up of differences and rivalries that were presented as the outcome of local disputes, most of which involved different ethnic groups. Ethnicity was indeed an additional characteristic of "neighborhood" life that had to be blunted in order to join up with "mainstream Israel," or "First Israel," as it was labeled in contrast to the "Second Israel" of the margins.

Ethnicity

Because of the great variety of ethnic origins among the neighborhood's residents, no single political dominance was expressed in ethnic terms. Apart from the Yemenites, who constituted the nucleus of the neighborhood's first inhabitants, no areas were identified according to the origin of their residents, owing to the desire to preserve the delicate balance between various areas of the neighborhood characterized by ethnic homogeneity. People were particularly careful not to connect political disputes with ethnic variance, and any attempt to do so was rejected. Nevertheless, the predominance of those of Oriental, and particularly Moroccan origin, left its mark on the structuring of residents' cultural identity. The status of the rehabilitation neighborhood, in which economic differences between residents were relatively small, taken together with its ethnic variety, provided evidence, in the words of one of the residents, that "we're all in the same boat and there is no-one to envy." Accusations of relative deprivation and discrimination according to the Oriental/Western (Sephardic/Ashkenazi) divide lost most of their sting, since it was the eastern European immigrants, most of whom were old and received welfare support, who occupied the bottom rung of the local economic ladder in the neighborhood. In addition to this, several of the local positions of power had for many years been in the hands of the Yemenite veterans, and if there was any sign of a political struggle couched in ethnic terms, it was between the old-time members of the neighborhood council in pre-project days, and a young generation, most of whom were involved in the Project and of second generation Moroccan origin.

Ethnicity was of value in presenting the neighborhood as a pluralistic cultural territory characterized by mutual respect, each part of which proudly preserving its traditional cuisine and dress for special occasions, such as the *Mimouna* celebrations at which, as in many other places, inter-ethnic brotherhood was advocated by way of publicly displaying a variety of presumably authentic ethnic folklore.

The City

The neighborhood was separated from its city center by a few kilometers of a mainly non-built-up area. A public transport service connected the neighborhood to the city; regular and frequent buses and taxis provided easy access to its shopping and entertainment centers. In addition, the neighborhood bordered on another residential area that was considered to be more affluent and was thus not included in Project Renewal. Nevertheless, the feeling of isolation among residents was widespread. They did not see themselves as residents of the city, but as residents of the neighborhood, and since convenient transportation was also available to the nearby metropolis of Tel Aviv, many of them preferred to do their shopping and to seek their entertainment in its anonymity, rather than being exposed in the city. The feeling of isolation was fueled in no small measure by the belief fostered by the local leadership that the neighborhood was greatly deprived with regard to the municipal distribution of resources. At the same time, many of the residents sought to improve their standard of living by moving to the city, and were extremely proud of the fact that another rehabilitation neighborhood in the same town was regarded as a failure, and that in comparison Arod was a symbol of success, both at the national and municipal levels. As was seen to be the case in all the previous images discussed, the attitude toward the city was ambivalent, incorporating contradictory attraction and rejection.

Community as Instant Acculturation

The following two instances portray two ways by which the neighborhood was cleansed of the life experiences of its residents. The first still maintains representational relationships with the neighborhood, whereas the second dispenses with them altogether and creates a simulation as an alternative to both the neighborhood and the residents. This political usage of a virtual community is highlighted here and contrasted with the neutral and taken-for-granted reference of sociologists to "communal webs" in Israel. *Communal Webs*, it should be noted, is the title of a collection of essays by Katriel (1989). The book presents various ethnographies of communication, ranging from the rhetorics of team spirit (*gibush*) to family picnics in military camps, whose over-arching context is the Israeli collectivity. The "communal webs" are described, in this book, without explicit reference to social groups—marginal or otherwise—that might suffer from or contest the workings of these "webs." In addition, these "webs" are given a firm, all-embracing cultural statute. They are presented as the contours of "the egg," rather than its disguises. The following two instances of manufacturing community, or weaving "communal webs" in an urban renewal area, focus not only on the "webs" but also on the spiders, namely the actors, ensnared in their own political agendas.

In order to mark the project's first anniversary, the project board met to discuss ways of celebrating the event. In contrast to the gravity and heated discussions that characterized other meetings, this one was conducted in a humorous vein and was devoid of tension. The participants, most of whom were residents of the neighborhood, made various light-hearted proposals as to "how to entertain our residents." Someone suggested a boxing contest, since "if they don't see blood they won't be satisfied." Another suggested a "Moroccan feast," because "that's what suits them and what they'll enjoy most." There was a general consensus that this type of entertainment would please the residents, attract an audience and meet their expectations. The initial proposals, however, which had obviously been made in jest, and betrayed more about attitudes toward the residents and the neighborhood than any intention of implementing them, were rejected. The reasons put forward for their rejection were of the kind that "the Project can't be identified with events such as these," and in particular: "Who can tell how the residents will behave? Perhaps they will go wild and run riot, and then what will we look like to the invited guests?" The consideration of the community's appearance to outsiders was sufficiently weighty to induce more serious suggestions. Thus, for example, the idea was put forward to invite the Pale Tracker (*Hagashash Hachiver*) entertainment group, well-known for its ethnic humor, "so that the residents can laugh at themselves a bit," but this was rejected because of the high cost involved.

Agreement was eventually reached on holding an exhibition of armaments to be set up by the army unit adopted by the residents, and on inviting a performance by The Natural Selection group, to be held at the center of town rather than in the neighborhood. This is a musical ensemble that strives to lend an authentic-classical air to Oriental music, thereby staking its claim to status and legitimacy in the field of serious music. The ensemble had won critical acclaim and recognition and was considered to be "civilized" entertainment as opposed to "cassette music" with which popular Oriental music is often identified in Israel. The choice of the city as the venue for the performance was not fortuitous either. The excuse that no suitable place was available was unconvincing, since well-attended events had taken place in the neighborhood, where a suitable hall had been found. The territorial detachment was part of the cultural isolation. Bringing Arod's residents to the city symbolized the neighborhood's abolition, both for its residents and the project team. The event was widely publicized, but demand for tickets was small, and much of the audience at the performance was made up of non-residents. The complete disappearance of the neighborhood and its residents will be demonstrated in the following, second instance, "an invitation to the community."

The inauguration ceremony for Arod's community center was held before a large gathering. Careful examination of the invitation sent to guests reveals some of the main characteristics of the concept of community and the ways of implementing it. Invitations were sent out to neighborhood notables, activists in Project Renewal, Jewish Agency officials, representatives of government ministries, senior municipal officials, and to many other guests from all parts of the country, and in particular to contributors from the sister city in the United States. The invitation's design indicates its purpose and significance. It was printed on top quality paper in Hebrew and in English. Apart from its value as a communication bridge between the two communities, the use of English establishes our community's standing within a wider, modern, Western and universal culture, one of whose ingredients is the English language. Thus, the neighborhood not only breaks out of the narrow confines of "Second Israel," but also extends beyond mainstream Israel and Israel altogether. With a mere wave of an invitation the neighborhood becomes part of the sought-after, rational, scientific, free and "(ac)cultured" world.

The invitation was headed by the emblems of the various bodies involved in establishing the center—first, the coat of arms of the city in which the center was located, followed by the insignia of the Jewish Agency, of the sister city abroad and finally of the neighborhood itself. The name attached to the illustration betrays the problematic nature of the center's essential function. In Hebrew it is called *Heichal Ha-tarbut veHa-sport* (palace of culture and sport), whereas in English it is simply a "community center." The Hebrew language imparts a combination of a "modern" meaning to the center ("culture and sport") and a religious one (*heichal*). This combination has become part of everyday speech, indicating a site for ongoing activity, unconditional of any specific time and place. The concept of "community," on the other hand, is identified with a given time and place, and as we have seen, the people of the neighborhood seek to break out of the problematic confines of their place and time, in other words, of the neighborhood.

As in other invitations to family events, such as weddings, circumcisions or bar mitzvas, the "parents/in-laws" also appear in Arod's invitation. In this case, these are the Jewish Agency, the municipality and the neighborhood committee together with the sister-city Jewish community. These three "take pleasure in inviting you to the inauguration ceremony of the Palace of Culture and Sport ———— which will take place on ————."

As in other family events, the inauguration ceremony is a rite of passage; that is, a festive-symbolic designation of the important and marked change that has taken place in the identity of the participants. During the ceremony outlined in the invitation, a neighborhood "becomes" a community. Yet this narrative of "becoming," rooted in the very essence of the project of "renewal," is actually a simulation, a staged production bearing little or no connection to the lived experience of residents.

During the inauguration ceremony, the heads of Project Renewal and its patrons made speeches before a selected audience, that had gained admittance to the grounds of the center by invitation only. An appropriate and evenly balanced audience was thus ensured, that could be relied upon not to disrupt the ceremony and to bring credit to the organizers. The *mezuzot* (parchment scrolls) were fixed in place amid much song and dance led by a well-known rabbi from another part of the country. This is an interesting fact, when one considers the large number of synagogues and rabbis available in the neighborhood. The invitation of a rabbi from the outside not only avoided local factionalism, but also imbued the neighborhood with an aura of belonging to the entire religious establishment. Following a tour of the building's components, in particular of the library, as befits a "palace of culture," groups of neighborhood women appeared before the guests, dressed in original ethnic attire. The picture was one of cultural diversity whose roots are not in the present, and which, moreover, presented the "authentic" people of the neighborhood as a piece of folklore. The gulf between the "exotic" apparel and ornaments and the modern, European dress of the visiting members of the American sister city community placed the former in the category of a museum exhibit, in contrast to the modern power and vitality of the latter. The image of this cultural subjugation was artistically formed during the following stage of the ceremony.

The program was presented to an invited local audience that filled the lavish hall to capacity at the beginning of the evening, but which steadily dwindled, with only a few people remaining to the end. This did not prevent the program running its full course. It included an appearance by the municipal orchestra, which set the seal of approval on the acceptance of the out-of-the-way neighborhood into the fold of the city to which it belonged. The inclusion of the neighborhood in the city was affirmed immediately afterward during a series of greetings and speeches made by the mayor, a senior government minister who read out a telegram of greeting from the prime minister, representatives of the neighborhood and of the Project, and a representative of the sister city. In the cultural performances that followed, the center's dancers appeared in jazz dance, devoid of any folkloric elements, while a local school choir sang songs from musicals, many of them from *Fiddler on the Roof.* The high point of the evening was a performance by a well-known singer who combined "good old Israeli" songs, with which the new community could now identify, with a visual "then and now" slide show. Pictures of the neighborhood's degenerate and neglected past were shown side by side with those portraying the present achievements of an exemplary, well-tended, clean and orderly place. The contrast was so blatant that there seemed to be no connection between the two periods, and the audience was no doubt torn between its degrading past as residents of an isolated neighborhood and the present, with its promise of a bright future as citizens of the nation, the country and the world. In fact, only a few of them remained in their seats to the end of the event. Most made their exit during the early stages of the evening, leaving behind them the youth-movement youngsters and the local hacks.

This vision of a future, utopian community created by the Project, spells the abolition of the neighborhood and its residents as a significant entity worthy of mirroring or even winking at, as was the case in the inauguration ceremony. It is also an abrogation of every system of symbols that connects the neighborhood and its residents to the concept of the community. The community has, in fact, become a self-display with no "self," a signifier with nothing signified, or in the words of Baudrillard, a simulation.

Afterword: Community as Simulation

This chapter followed Anderson's (1983) logic of the "imagining of community," with a significant addition: the community described here was imagined at the expense of a rich ethnic heritage. The community as instant acculturation could be expected to work only through the abolition of the neighborhood with its ethnic stigma. The rite of transition, operated by Ashkenazi officials and their Sephardi "sidekicks," demanded that the Sephardi inmates are first stripped of their Sephardi identity. In that sense, it perpetuated the original discrimination with which Sephardi immigrants were confronted in Ashkenazi Israel.

The enactment of community as described here, like the story of the "disguised egg" with which the book opened, illustrates not successful acculturation but the opposite—namely the collapse of the ideology of acculturation, the bankruptcy of the dream that a new culture can be freely imposed on some passive recipients. The story of modernization, so often told by anthropologists and "project renewal" officers alike, appears in Arod as an ideological facade, remote from the everyday experience of "the residents" subjected to it. This is seen most blatantly from the point of view of reception: as the "community anniversary" demonstrated, only the narrative of presentation remained while the audience (literally) disappeared. This disappearance metaphorically equals the abolition of the Sephardi subject as part and parcel of the Ashkenazi attempt to resolve the discourse of social inequalities.

This critical point of view, as I pointed out in the introduction, is largely missing from the socio-anthropological discourse on Israel. Broadly speaking, the Israeli collective memory is a similar, though much more elaborate, "invitation to community"—a canonical text cleansed of marginal subjects. In spite of the variety and richness to be found in Israeli society, anthropologists researching it have largely refrained from elucidating the views of residents regarding their "culture," and invariably have not attempted to describe acculturation as a playful, winking performance, or (even worse), an empty simulation.[3] In contrast, anthropologists (in Israel and elsewhere) largely imposed their own serious view, their own functional narrative of acculturation-as-development. For these reasons, I think that what happened in Arod (and other deprived settings of "Second Israel") can be better and differently understood using simulation as the analytic frame.

Furthermore, the example of Arod illustrates some of the ways in which youth is both targeted and appropriated by adults in the context of the ethnic cleavage in Israel. In a nutshell, the treatment of youth represents a double-edged usurpation. On the one hand, youngsters who do not live up to their community's expectations are "a mark of Cain"; on the other hand, the youngsters are represented as the most creative, fresh and unspoiled component of the community. As progeny, youth is inadvertently placed in the buffer zone between present and future, here and there, and—in the context of the ethnic cleavage—"us" (Sepharadim) and "them" (Ashkenazim). For example, when some of the local youngsters were not drafted into the army on grounds of social incompatibility this became a sore point, about which Arod's adults were embarrassed. A television documentary portraying the arduous and tortuous process of an Arod youngster's acceptance to an army unit was conceived by residents as a mark of Cain on the neighborhood's forehead. It drew attention to the neighborhood, but the wrong kind of attention. On the other hand, Arod's youth were the real stars of the community festival. In the cultural performances during the anniversary, young dancers appeared in jazz—not folk—dances, and a local school choir sang songs from *Fiddler on the Roof.* The community therefore showed off with its "Westernized," acculturated youth. The true voice of the youngsters themselves was, of course, never heard during this simulation of community.

In the following chapter I turn to discuss another collectivist script of "acculturation" that can be described as a rite of initiation for Israeli youth into national culture. It is the story of how the Israeli school system prepares its students for their meeting with the Holocaust.

NOTES

1. The popular employment of the concept of "community" in Arod was not very far from its appropriation within the more "scientific discourse" of sociology. "Community," although regarded as a sociological unit of analysis and comparison, is in fact a mixture of commonly accepted denotation and lack of definiteness, of international meaning (Warren 1973; Schneider 1979) as well as unique locality (Cohen 1982). The rhetorical nature of "community" may well render it analytically questionable, turning "community studies" into a myth, as Stacy (1969) suggested. One wonders what would be the results of employing a similar, critical analysis toward the recent rhetorical upsurge about "communitarianism" in America.

2. The principle of "adoption" by a sister-city community from the diaspora was one of Project Renewal's innovations, and enabled direct transfer of funds to the adopted community, and active participation on the part of the adopting community in the physical and social planning and in the distribution of resources in the locality.

3. For example, the wink of self-awareness and the political use of social amnesia can be revealed in ceremonial revelry and saintly cults, so often discussed in Israeli anthropology as functional symbols of "authentic," (counter-)cultural identity. An analysis of this sort is already concealed between the pages of the research by Bilu and Ben-Ari (1992) by the creation of "cults of the righteous" by the Abu-Hatsera family. Or, the alternative interpretation proposed here can be used to show how birthday celebrations in kindergartens are not only "functional national ceremonies of socialization" but mainly a game (see Shamgar-Handelman and Handelman 1991; Weil 1986). Likewise, the element of simulation present in community singing among Israeli ?migr?s in New York, seen by Shokeid (1990) as a functional resort from cultural alienation, can be thrown into relief. A similar Baudrillardian simulation is associated with the practical Bible lessons attended by ultra-orthodox women, seriously interpreted by El-Or (1990) as a functional gender socialization mechanism. Such an alternative view can elucidate the well-developed self-awareness, among these women, of the paradoxes that create their status. Only moderate theoretical flexibility is required to demonstrate that the revelations of Moroccan dreamers (Bilu and Abramovitch 1985), the religious lessons in Jerusalem (Heilman 1983), or the structuring of the past by residents of an old-age home (Hazan 1992) do not conform to traditional representational relationships with the surrounding reality, and that an association of simulation would afford just as good an understanding of them as does the usual symbolic relation.

2. REVISING THE HOLOCAUST
The Historical Discourse

*M*ore than fifty years after the defeat of Nazi Germany, the memory of the Holocaust is very much alive in Israel. This memory came under a full-blown attack in 1988, when a well-known Israeli intellectual, Yehouda Elkana, published an opinion article titled "In Favor of Forgetting."[1] The article, which stirred much controversy, argued that Israeli leaders should refrain from overemphasizing the lessons of the Holocaust and instead focus their attention on the living people and their future. It was written in the emotionally loaded context of John Demyaniuk's trial coupled with the first months of the Palestinian uprising (*Intifada*). The trial and the *Intifada*, according to Elkana, were not entirely a coincidence; rather, both signified a certain persistent interpretation of the Holocaust in Israel, resulting in a deep anxiety and a victimization complex. Elkana argued that the Holocaust can yield no positive lessons. The world may need to remember, but Israel must forget in order to become "normal," rid itself of its siege mentality.

Elkana's argument opens a window to the problematic place of "the Holocaust" in Israeli collective memory. Forgetting the Holocaust is no less a significant issue than commemorating it. In fact, Elkana's words should remind us that social amnesia is always a part of collective memory, and can be just as contrived and conscious. Replying to

Elkana, Zukerman (1988–89) agreed that Israeli society has reified the Holocaust as a rhetorical ritual of nationalism. Yet, as he points out, in doing this, Israel in fact did not commemorate "the Holocaust," but rather a priori repressed it and appropriated its mythical image as an instrumental affirmation of its own militaristic disposition. Putting the Jews back in history—the goal of the Zionist project—necessitated the construction of the Holocaust as myth. Zukerman therefore suggested that we need to return to a more true and concrete chronicle of the Holocaust, for example the detailed record offered by Lantzman in his film *Shoa'a* (Holocaust). The question is, evidently, if such an option is at all feasible, or whether collective memories are already, ipso facto, recycled as myths and ideologies.

The myth of the Holocaust has had a key role in the shaping of Israeli national identity ever since the inception of the state. During the last decade, third-generation Israeli-born pupils have been revisiting sites of the Holocaust through school delegations headed to the concentration camps in Poland. Established around 1985, school delegations have become tremendously popular. Delegations are now formed not only under the auspices of the Ministry of Education, but also by youth movements and independent schools. Private tourist agencies offer "concentration camps tours," complete with guides and hotel booking. Roughly estimated, the number of pupils who have participated in such excursions over the decade reaches over fifty thousand. Born out of a sincere need of pupils to see for themselves the realities of the Holocaust, delegations also have become an ideological tool for inducing certain worldviews. Studying these Holocaust delegations therefore allows us to reassess the social meanings and uses of the Holocaust in contemporary Israel. The delegations provide a window into how Israeli society remembers and learns to forget.

The Holocaust in Israeli Eyes:
A Brief History of Collective Images

The Holocaust delegations studied here[2] are unique. Jews are not the only people to have died in the camps, but such delegations do not exist in European countries and only Israel has formally instituted such massive pilgrimage to the camps. Furthermore, Israeli delegations are not composed exclusively of grandchildren of Holocaust survivors; there is a rather large percentage (though smaller than 50 percent) of delegates who have no family history related to the Holocaust, for example, pupils of Sephardic origin.

The Holocaust is no doubt a key symbol of Israeli identity (Young 1988; Bar-On and Sela 1991). This is due to the sheer enormity of events, the great proportion of Holocaust survivors in Israel (nearly half the population in 1948) and the negative place of the Holocaust in Zionist ideology as the ultimate consequence of Jewish vulnerability in the diaspora. The few sites of ghetto uprisings have been over-emphasized in Israel so as to fit into the frame of a national "hero-system." Yet the majority of Jewish Holocaust victims proved to be a persistent problem in historical interpretation and commemoration. The following concise description of phases in the history of the Holocaust should illustrate the various ways in which this problem has been approached.

The pre-state's reactions to the Holocaust reflected, to a large extent, a sense of resentment about the behavior of Jewish victims. These, according to the widely held belief, passively accepted their fate and subscribed to the traditional, passive Jewish line of conduct in the diaspora (Liebman and Don-Yehia 1983; Porat 1986). An Israeli paratrooper returning from Hungary in 1945 reported that in Tel-Aviv he was repeatedly asked "Why didn't the Jews rebel? Why did they go as lambs to slaughter?" (Palgi 1978:243). It was around this period that the nickname "soap" was coined and used widely in reference to Holocaust survivors (Segev 1991:167; Firer 1989:53). This stance, representing an Israeli desire to dissociate from Holocaust victims, emerged from the socialist-Zionist ideological rejection of the Jewish diaspora, together with ideas of militarism and state-sovereignty turned into a way of life in Israel (Ben-Eliezer 1988; Zerubavel 1995). In a Kibbutz *Haggada* (a secular version of the Passover Haggada written and read by members of Kibbutzim) written just after the Holocaust, it was argued that "not only Hitler is responsible for the death of the six millions— but all of us—and first and foremost these six millions. Had they known that a Jew has power too, they would not have all gone as lamb to slaughter" (Reich 1972:393).

The metaphor of "lamb to the slaughter" denotes a negative ideological predilection rather than a factual state-of-affairs. Originally a biblical metaphor (Jesi 53:7), "lamb to slaughter" became, for Israelis, the cumulative conception of what was considered as the Jews' passive acceptance of their victimization, from the Middle Ages crusades to Kishinev's pogroms. Some prayers of *kaddish* (traditional prayer for the dead) written especially in memory of the victims of the Holocaust, formerly included the words "lambs to slaughter." Some of these texts were given to school delegates of the Israeli Ministry of Education for reading at ceremonies (Segev 1991:453).

Alongside the passive image of lamb to the slaughter, an opposite image of the Holocaust Jew also emerged during that period: the Jew as rebel. The general Holocaust memorial day is held annually on the date of the Warsaw ghetto uprising, and is officially titled "Holocaust and Heroism Day," heroism meaning the militant act of uprising. During the 1950s and 1960s there was an overemphasis on active resistance, and those who resisted were usually represented as belonging to Zionist youth movements. The Holocaust was absent from the normal curriculum until the 1970s; afterwards, early Israeli educational texts dealing with it have replaced, when referring to the rebels, the word "Jews" by "Hebraic" (Ivrim) and "sons of Israel" (Firer 1989).

In the first period, beginning from 1945, Holocaust Jews were therefore perceived as the "antithesis of the self-image that has been inculcated into Israeli collective identity" (Carmon 1988:76). The Holocaust, respectively, was seen as a point of departure from Jewish history, a culmination of the diaspora from which Israel broke away and dissociated itself. The diaspora, which culminated in the Holocaust, represented one history line; Zionism represented another. The major proponent of this stance was David Ben-Gurion, Israel's first prime minister. Ben-Gurion's doctrine of state-sovereignty rejected the Holocaust as irrelevant to Israeli reality. To Ben-Gurion (1957), the Holocaust was something which "happened to the diaspora Jews because they were diaspora Jews," and "antisemitism, the Dreyfus trial, Jewish persecutions in Rumania ... are for us events from foreign history and sad memories of the diaspora Jews, but not a spiritual experience nor life facts of instructive value." In an interview to the *New York Times* (18.12.60) made before the Eichmann trial, Ben-Gurion justified the trial as "proving to Israel's younger generation that Israelis are not like lambs to be taken to slaughter, but a nation able of fighting back."

The Eichmann trial, itself a demonstration of Israel's power, also had the effect of reintroducing the Holocaust into the public agenda. Extensive testimonies of Holocaust survivors were broadcast nationwide, replacing the former dissociation from and silencing of these survivors. Following the Eichmann trial, during the 1970s and the beginning of the 1980s, the stance toward Holocaust survivors was gradually changing. This change was precipitated by two wars, the Six-Day War (1967) and the October, or Yom-Kippur War (1973), which shook the traditional Israeli worldview. These wars emphasized, to both Israelis and Jews abroad, the fragile existence of Israel, its solitude (especially in the waiting period before June 1967) and dependence on external, especially American, help (for example, the airlift aid provided by the U.S. during the first weeks of the October War).

Following these wars, the Holocaust again became relevant to Israeli reality, and was redefined as the ultimate expression of the evil intents of the Gentiles and their everlasting Jews-hatred (Liebman and Don-Yehia 1983). The Holocaust was molded as a constant reminder to "what happened and can happen anew." In a memorial ceremony to the Holocaust held in 1976, Golda Meir said that "the Holocaust of each and every Jew has become the collective Holocaust for the state of Israel" (*Ma'ariv* 27.4.76), and Gideon Hausner, former prosecutor in the Eichmann trial (1960) stated that "the Holocaust and the rebels are still part of our reality" (ibid.). A major proponent of this vantage was Menachem Begin (prime minister of the Likud Party), who in the middle of the Lebanon war, during the Siege on Beirut, described Ya'ser Arafat as a "Hitler hiding in the bunker" from the Israeli soldiers (*Ye'diot Acharonot* 4.8.82). This interpretation redefined the Holocaust as a national integrating factor and a locus of Jewish solidarity. It later resurfaced in a similar and powerful way during the Gulf War (Zukerman 1993).

The ideological changes just described were also apparent in the educational system. In the 1970s, teaching the Holocaust was first introduced at schools. A new approach to the Jewish behavior during the Holocaust has emerged: *Amida* (stand), emphasizing that survival under the Nazis demanded a "spiritual resistance" which was just as active. The word *Gevura* (heroism) was removed, during that time, from the name of the Holocaust Memorial Day. In 1979, the Ministry of Education invited two curricular programs devoted exclusively to the Holocaust (Carmon 1980; Gutman and Shatzker 1983).

These cumulative changes brought about the third and current phase. This phase may be dated from 1990, in which the Holocaust Memorial Day was replaced by the memorial project of "To Everyone There is a Name" (the public reading of the list of names of Holocaust victims). Instead of the stereotypical and generalized images of the "lamb to the slaughter" and "the rebel," this project invited passersby to read, through a loudspeaker, the names of Holocaust victims in various posts erected throughout the country. It was only in this third stage, and with the third generation, that Israeli society has reconsidered the Holocaust predominantly in terms of the suffering of the individual.

The current phase is characterized by pluralist approaches to the Holocaust, rather than a monolithic ideology of rejection/integration. Part of this "multi-vocality" stems from the fact that the Israeli establishment has lost the central hegemonic place it had enjoyed during the early days of nation-building (first phase). Other signs of this multi-vocality of the third phase are, for example, the plurality of literary poetics of the Holocaust (Raz 1994) and the upsurge of critical historical/sociological readings of the relationship between Israelis and Holocaust Jews (for example, Porat 1986; Segev 1991; Sivan 1991).

The School Delegations

Rather than purporting to examine the delegates "before" and "after," the Holocaust tour was studied as a continuum of three phases: the preparations, the journey, and the return to school. The resulting report focuses on the preparatory stage, in which the ideological framework of the delegation is laid out and inculcated upon both teachers and pupils. Fieldwork for this study was conducted in Israel in 1995. It focused on the Ministry of Education's preparatory course for delegation chaperon-teachers (teachers authorized to chaperon the Ministry's delegations), as well as on three Israeli schools conducting preparations for a delegation. Following is a brief description of these two research arenas.

The ministry's course is conducted, in recent years, from January to June, one full day (eight hours) per week. Most of the meetings are held in the ministry's instruction center in Petach-Tikva, a city in the center of Israel. Some meetings take place in well-known national centers for the commemoration and teaching of the Holocaust, such as Yad Vashem (The Holocaust Martyrs' and Heroes' Remembrance Authority in Jerusalem) and Beit Lochamei Hageta'ot (in Hebrew, the House of Ghetto Warriors"; located in kibbutz Yad Mordechai). The course is usually given to some 20 to 30 participants selected by the ministry's "Poland committee" from roughly 100 applicants. All applicants must have a teaching diploma and their application must be signed by their school's principal. Following the course, participants conduct a nine-day visit to Poland.

In the case of the ministry's course, the study was primarily faced with a problem of access. My research assistant applied to the Poland Committee in order to participate in the course, but was rejected on the grounds that (a) he is not a teacher, and (b) all academic research on the delegations is in the hands of the ministry and should be properly considered and licensed by the ministry's research authorities. As a result, we informally approached several teachers who formerly undertook the ministry's course, and—with their informed consent—interviewed them and read the notes they took during the course. Later, archive work led us to documents relating to the course, such as formal schedules, summaries and reports written by the ministry's officials and by the course academic advisor. There was much to be learned about the course from these sources, and this was complemented by participant observation of the actual preparations for the delegation, which took place at schools.

For this purpose, three schools were chosen. First, a state-secular high school in a central Israeli city which will be called Dahar. Second, a high school in the Galilee belonging to the kibbutz educational system; and third, a high school in Tel-Aviv belonging to the state-religious educational stream. While all schools were recognized by the Ministry of Education, they also represented different sections in the ministry, thus allowing for an ideological comparison.[3] The schools' delegates were 11-grads or 12-grads, and the eight-day delegation was usually scheduled for April, during the Passover school break, so as not to lose school days. Preparations for the delegation usually began around January, although this differed among schools. Preparations were composed of after-school meetings and organized visits to Holocaust museums and memorials. This was complemented by a regular history class focusing on the Holocaust.

The Ministry's Course

Held for eight hours each Thursday from January to June, the 1994 course included about 25 participants. The course program was composed of lectures on four subjects, in the following order. First, Poland: general history—divided in two periods, until World War I, and between World War I and World War II; the Polish people—culture and religion; and Poland during World War II. Second, the Jews in Poland: the Rabbinical establishment; the *chasidut* (Jewish mystical movement); Polish Jews in the nineteenth century; Polish Jews between the world wars. Third, Nazism: "From Antisemitism to Nazi Ideology," "The Nazi Policy towards the Jews." Fourth, the Holocaust: "The Ghettos—An Overview"; "Concentration and Labor Camps"; "The

Reinhard Operation"; "The Warsaw Ghetto"; "Everyday Life in the Warsaw Ghetto"; The Krakov Ghetto"; "Lublin"; "Maidanek"; "Auschwitz"; "The Person in the Camp"; "Youth Movements: From Clubs to Underground"; "Rebellion and Standing (Hebrew: *Amida*)"; "The Krakov Resistance"; "The Motif of Honor in the Call to Rebellion"; and, finally, "The Righteous among the Nations in The Holocaust"[4] and "The Partisan Movement in Poland." The last two meetings of the course were dedicated to an open panel on the "Polish-Jewish Dialogue after the Holocaust" (the panel included a Polish scholar), and an open discussion on "The Journey to Poland as Moral Education: Human, Jewish and Israeli Existence after the Holocaust." Lectures were given during the morning and afternoon; the last part of the day was dedicated to more instrumental sessions, called workshops, which dealt with topics such as school preparations, emotional reactions, preparing the camp ceremonies, etc. Some of these preparations will be illustrated during the next section, which deals with the actual school preparations.

The course program reveals a rich variety of topics with a focus on the Holocaust. "Holocaust heroism" is there, but so are the partisans or Poland's general history. It is a pluralistic program which does not disclose any exclusive ideological predilection. The program also included visits to Yad Vashem, the House of Ghetto Warriors, and watching the film *Der Ewige Jude* (The Eternal Jew)—an antisemitic film produced in Germany in 1941.

In addition to attending lectures and workshops, participants had to prepare three assignments during the course: (1) a paper on one of the sites or topics included in the journey's schedule, (2) a teacher's guide for one of the sites, and (3) a complete teacher's guide for the journey, as the course's term paper. Participants later told me that these assignments, which they often did in groups, were very useful. They expressed a positive view regarding the course program and goals. This is perhaps not surprising, taking into account the fact that all participants were in the first place interested to take part in this course and had to undergo a process of selection. The criticism expressed regarded missing aspects in the course's program, such as "lectures on art, Jewish and Polish art, as well as a lecture on Holocaust Hebrew literature." Others positively recalled the insistence on punctual arrival and presence in the course meetings. Again, this is perhaps not surprising, taking into account that all participants were high-school teachers.

School Preparations

School delegations to Poland have existed for ten years under the auspices of the Ministry of Education's special project, titled "Looking for My Brothers" and initiated under Minister Yizchak Navon (Labor Party). Since 1986 the ministry has also supervised the "March of the Living," in which thousands of Jewish adolescents from around the world walk from Birkenau to Auschwitz. Before the delegations were institutionalized, local kibbutz delegations had taken place as early as the beginning of the 1980s, when Poland resumed its diplomatic relations with Israel. In fact, the first delegations had gone out in the 1960s, but were stopped as a result of the cutting of diplomatic ties by Poland after the Six-Day War. One of the early delegates, returning from Poland in 1966, said it was only "there that I understood the meaning of homeland, heroism, and the Jewish tragedy.... There I found the answer to the question that always bothered me, why did Jews go as lambs to slaughter? The answer was in the blood stains of the victims, which I saw on the grounds of the camp, in the power of the Nazi death machine and the great misleading performed by Nazis" (Frishman 1966). The same rhetoric would repeat itself 25 years later. In 1988, the ministry published a special general memorandum titled "Criteria and Instructions for the Approvement of Delegations to Poland." This memorandum was the earliest statement of the pedagogic rationale for the delegation. "We regard these delegations," it states, "as an experience touching the depths of the soul and conveying emotions deeper than words of glorious Jewish life demolished by the hands of the killers.... Our pupils will return from this journey with a strengthened sense of belonging to the history and legacy of the Jewish people." This memorandum was written under Minister Zevulun Hammer, member of the national-religious party (*Mafdal*). It expresses a certain worldview in which Jewish identity is emphasized. Later, as the minister changed, so did the emphasis.

The same memorandum also details how to prepare the delegates. These directives later became the general framework for the ministry's course as well as for school preparations. It instructs schools to "conduct 4–6 months of preparation in which the delegates will be accompanied by a special teacher who has been trained in the ministry's course as well as by a testimony person who will also participate in the delegation itself." This "testimony person" is a Holocaust survivor who gives talks before the journey and joins the delegation in Poland to provide on-the-spot explanations. "Preparation should also include visits to authorized Holocaust museums and memorials such as Yad Vashem, The House of Ghetto Warriors, etc." The ministry recommends to prepare a "journey handbook" which will include "details of destinations, short summaries of the preparation, maps and diagrams, ceremonial readings and other reading excerpts." These journey handbooks, issued by the ministry as well as by related educational authorities and youth movements, had to capture the essence of the Holocaust as it should be presented to the delegates. They hence came to embody an ideological narrative of the Holocaust, on which I will later focus. In the remaining part of its memorandum, the ministry recommends that the journey will be made to Poland alone, "so as to deepen the effect." It suggests that pupils should participate in the delegations only according to their own will. Finally, it is recommended that delegates work in "the cleaning and rehabilitation of Jewish commemorative sites in Poland." The ministry's recommended journey schedule is for nine days including Treblinka, the Warsaw ghetto, Auschwitz-Birkenau, Krakov, and Maidanek-Lublin. The ministry's delegations are expected to fly only with the national Israeli airline, "El-Al."

Dahar School and State Ideology

One of the informants in Dahar School was a senior female teacher called Nadia (all names are fictive). Besides her regular job as a history teacher, Nadia was also responsible for the delegation's preparation. Rina was a junior female teacher and the current delegation chaperon.

NADIA: In 1988 I chaperoned the first delegation from Dahar School. This year, for the first time, we go out on our own, with about 60 students. We wanted to give every student who wanted it the opportunity to go. The ministry restricted the number to 32 students. We already knew how to prepare, since we have been doing it under the guidance of the ministry for so long. The school will also choose and send a testimony person with the delegation on the school's expense.

RINA: Already in the beginning of the year, pupils started to ask us what about Poland, and parents came to me and said: "You remember that my son went in the delegation last year, this year my daughter wants to go...." We felt we couldn't refuse them. Why refuse them? They will pay for the journey.

NADIA: The whole thing had grown enormously. Every year there are more applications. We did not want to employ selection, I even hesitate to use this word in this context. We would have had even more delegates, but the matriculation exam in chemistry is held just after the return of the delegation.

RINA: After the applications came in, we met with the future delegates for a preliminary meeting. We put a large piece of paper on the floor and each pupil wrote his or her expectations from the journey, from themselves, and from the chaperons. In my group there were many third generations. Most of them focused on the expectations they had concerning themselves. Namely, that they will "pass" the journey and become better persons, better Israelis. They wrote that they would like their friends to be supportive and their teacher to be like one of the guys.

During the first meeting, which was also attended by parents, Rina read an excerpt from a text written by a Dahar graduate who went to Poland in a previous delegation.

Now that I returned, I know why I went there. I looked for the roots of the Jewish people, the millions that were killed. The future is built on the past, and if we forget the past, we end by repeating what happened there. I personally promise not to forget. I have returned different: full of pride to belong to the state of Israel. Who would have believed that us pupils would fight for the opportunity to hold up the Israeli flag? It happened in Poland. You had to see it in order to believe. People walking three kilometers with the flag raised high in their hand, refusing to give it away. You had to be there, in order to understand that the only place for Jews is the state of Israel.

When asked about possible ideological bias in the preparation, Dahar teachers commented that in their opinion, if there was such ideological bias, it did not play a dominant role. "We try to prepare them for the experience by giving as much information beforehand as possible," Rina said, "it's the ministry that chooses which information is to be presented." However, it was Rina who chose the above cited letter. In order to grasp the role of ideology, one has to go directly to the most significant texts used during the preparation, namely the journey handbooks. A critical reading of these reveals the same nationalistic narrative which underpinned the letter of the ex-delegate chosen to be read at the first meeting.

During preparations, an extensive use was made of two older handbooks. The first, written for a previous delegation from Tel-Aviv state-secular schools, was titled *Handbook of the Holocaust and Heroism*. It opens with the following letter from the mayor of Tel-Aviv: "Poland is the most tragic example of the impossibility of Jewish existence without a homeland. In that sense it is also the most convincing evidence for the basic truth of Zionism" (Lahat, journey handbook of the Tel-Aviv municipal delegation, 1988). This quote expresses the Zionist world-view in which the Holocaust justifies, indeed necessitates, a strong state of Israel. The motivation behind studying the "Jewish history that existed in Poland for a thousand years until its total destruction" is but one: the understanding that Jews must have a homeland, that is, the internalization of the categorical need in Israel. "There is no Jewish existence without a homeland." This is the realization of Ben-Gurion's doctrine of state-sovereignty explicated in the introduction to this chapter. On the other hand, it can also be related to the writer's mili-tary and political background. However, similar writings are found in the preparatory texts of the ministry itself. For example, consider the following excerpts, which were also used in the preparation: "If there is a meaning to the journey to Poland, it is first and foremost to empha-sis our Israeliness and a total negation of the diaspora, which we tend to legitimize these days" (David Kochavi, from the ministry's handbook titled *Looking for My Brothers*).

Following Lahat's letter there was another letter, written by the aca-demic advisor of the ministry's course. This letter brings a much softer, academic version of the ministry's worldview. It urges readers to remem-ber the "Jewish legacy" alongside its "destruction in the Holocaust" and to consider the "Nazi cruelty" side by side with the "human sparkles of the righteous among the nations." The concluding message is contained in the last sentence. "One of the pupils who returned from Poland," it reads, "said: 'I hope I returned a better Jew.' His friend added: 'I hope I returned a better person.'" With this proclamation the letter ends. The Dahar pupils discussed it, and concluded that the opposition is left intentionally unresolved, as if the dilemma should be decided anew by each delegate. This is the neutral, pluralist, humanistic worldview of the Holocaust, as the academic advisor would probably like to see it.

RINA: In the second meeting, we showed a film by Helena Birenbaum called Life as Hope, on life in the ghetto. Then pupils met with a testimony person and with Yurek, a survivor from the Warsaw ghetto. Then they had a lecture on the Polish-Jews relations since 1000 A.C. The lecturer described the Poles as basically good people who were driven to do what they did, and this provoked many angry reactions from pupils.

An apparent gap poses itself between the pedagogic rationale of the ministry's course and the actual preparations and reactions of pupils as well as teachers. The former seeks to develop pluralism, tolerance and universal as well as Israeli lessons; the latter stick to the narrower interpretation of the Holocaust as justifying and necessitating a strong state of Israel. This gap is especially significant in the case of a state-secular school, which is most directly influenced by the ministry's directives.

Galilee School—Kibbutzim's Educational Framework

In 1994 a kibbutz regional school in Galilee began a new preparation program for its Poland delegation. This program was scheduled to take a whole year, rather than the ministry's four months, and to begin in the eleventh grade. The program drew on the kibbutzim's journey handbook from 1987, as outlined below.

In spring 1987 a large kibbutzim delegation went to Poland. Their journey handbook includes several unique features. First, it has a general description of Poland, focusing on industrialization. Titled "Industrialization as the No. 1 Economic Goal of Poland," the piece gives a detailed introduction of the "Nova Huta" steel plants near Krakov and about the competition between independent Polish farmers and the government's subsidized farms. This economic focus no doubt reflects the kibbutzim's own economic concerns regarding industrialization and government agricultural policy. Following this economic introduction, there is a political overview, headed by a section titled "Poland's Relations with the USSR." This emphasis, absent in other handbooks, is also part of the kibbutzim's socialist worldview and concerns. In an interview with Gil, one of the Galilee school's chaperon-teachers, he told me that

> when one escorts several consecutive delegations, as a teacher, one becomes aware of the waking up of these formerly Communist countries. In many places in Poland, for example, you see shops where once there was nothing to drink or eat. Unfortunately, pupils cannot witness these changes because they go only once. But I, as a teacher, try to open their eyes to the larger context of our journey. Europe was not frozen since the Holocaust, remaining as is until 1995. It has changed.

Back in 1987, Poland was preoccupied with the still-underground activities of the Polish workers' movement "Solidarity," headed by Lech Valensa. The 1987 handbook refers to Solidarity as "the movement which should not be named." "The churches' backyards are filled with the movement's activity and the name of the man from Gdansk is written on the walls." This intriguing self-censorship is possibly meant to generate interest among readers. The emphatic, mysteriously romantic description of "the Movement" is arguably geared to evoke identification with a socialist Proletariat movement whose goals resemble the traditional, avant-garde ideology of the kibbutzim. Other general references to Poland include maps and a list of "historical figures," among them King Michiko I, Queen Yadwena, Mari Kiri, the first Polish pope, the pianist Pederewski, Joseph Konrad, Schopen and Copernicus.

Part of the Galilee school's new program was a focus on a special theme for the delegation; for example, "fifty years after the Nazi occupation of Hungary." This theme is changed each year, and themes belong to the realm of general history rather than to Jewish or Israeli identity. The kibbutz program and handbook therefore embody several important differences from the program and handbooks of the state-secular schools. These differences are apparently aimed at a more general knowledge of Poland, Europe, and the changes they have been going through. In fact, the kibbutz program can be seen, in this respect, to resemble the pedagogic rationale of the ministry's course.

GIL: Kibbutzim, like everyone else, define themselves through education, and the education for the delegation is part of that. The fact that we constructed a special kibbutz preparatory program shows you that we are not satisfied with the ministry's program.

Gil's comment was said during an open discussion with the classroom, and pupils felt free to join in the conversation.

PUPIL A: It's like the Kibbutz Haggadah written after World War II. That was also different.

GIL: Yes, with a major difference. Some Haggadah written in kibbutzim treated Holocaust victims as lambs to slaughter. Nowadays we self-criticize this conception.

PUPIL B: We're different from other delegations, that's clear. Just think how we are responsible for financing our journey by working in other kibbutzim. This happens only in the kibbutz. Other delegates are subsidized by the ministry and by their parents.

Another interesting feature of the kibbutz's preparations is the relative absence of an emphasis on "Holocaust heroism," a subject which is given prominence in the ministry's directive to "experience and try to comprehend the full meaning of the brave and unconditional fight of the Jews who rebelled against the Nazi killers" (the Ministry's General Memorandum, 1988). However, this aspect was well-emphasized in the preparations and handbooks of other kibbutzim delegations, that were formed within the kibbutz youth movement rather than at school.

One such youth movement, called *Hashomer Hatzair* (The Young Guard), has its own preparation course, journey handbook and journey schedule. For example, the list of sites to be visited by *Hashomer Hatzair* in Warsaw contains six (out of nine) places connected either to the Warsaw ghetto uprising or the socialist youth movement. A detailed description of these sites is found in the handbook. It is absent from all other handbooks. The emphasis, it should be pointed out, is actually not on "Jewish heroism" but on the part that the Zionist, socialist youth movement had in the uprising. This is the heritage which *Hashomer Hatzair* has (rightfully or otherwise) appropriated. The handbook also includes a text called "The Day's Command in 18 Mila Street," composed by Aba Kovner, a famous *Hashomer Hatzair* persona and formerly the commander of the Vilna ghetto uprising.

> In this place where your feet are now treading, unfolded one of the most unbelievable epics in the history of Israel and of Mankind.... Here, in this bunker, the remaining rebels were killed. We are still grieving this terrible tragedy that happened here and on all of Europe's land. But we are allowed to feel pride when we remember Mordechai Anilevitz, the Warsaw ghetto uprising commander, and his fellow warriors.... In these days *Hakkibutz Ha'artzi* [historically the more leftist of the kibbutzim movement, to which Hashomer Hatzair is related as a youth movement] marks its sixtieth anniversary. In anniversaries, all those who respect their heritage establish orders of honor and bestow titles of nobility to those who are found worthy. From all the existing titles of nobility, the most noble and committing one is to continue the legacy of Anilevitz and his brothers in arms, and their vision of salvation.

A teacher involved in the preparations of *Hashomer Hatzair* delegates told me that what they do is "a pilgrimage to our legacy of heroism." In this respect, *Hashomer Hatzair* is an extreme realization of the Zionist-secular state-sovereignty worldview, which seeks to emphasize its activist Israeli identity through the negation of the diaspora and the "Holocaust Jew." In the case of *Hashomer Hatzair*, the diaspora has been arguably forgotten and deleted, symbolically replaced by the heroic rebels, the founding fathers of this youth movement.

The Tel-Aviv School—State-Religious Education

The preparations of the state-religious school offered completely different educational contents. The difference took shape not only in contents but also through language. The whole grammar, the linguistic world of idioms, was different. The preparation for the journey, for example, was called a "seminar" rather than a "delegation." Current seminars draw heavily on a 1988 seminar handbook titled *In the Shadow of the Scaffolds*. The 1988 handbook opens with a biblical motto, "The secret of salvation is in remembrance." Next is a letter from the religious-national youth movement's chairperson, whose opening lines are "Dear friends, may the God of Israel be with you." Asaf, a chaperon-teacher in Tel-Aviv school, explained the preparations as focusing on "telling the pupils about the difficult experience of the journey—how we are going to walk in *Stetels* (Jewish ruined diaspora communities), in small alleys and among demolished buildings, trying to capture a sense of what was there, of the Jewish life that once flourished in Poland."

Capturing the Jewish life that once flourished in Poland: this is indeed the key to the religious-state preparations. Preparations here take a shorter period, an intensive week to three-week long "seminar" whose exclusive focus is on Jewish life. There were no visits to the House of Ghetto Warriors, indeed no mention of "Holocaust heroism." There was one visit to Yad Vashem, and to the religious museum of the Holocaust in *martef Zion* (Zion's Cellar). The fact that pupils are already familiar with "Jewish life," while other, more general topics are avoided, perhaps accounts for the short preparations. The identification with Jewish life in Poland, as inculcated during the preparations, is an unconditional one, stemming from a common Jewish identity. Dorit, a delegate in Tel-Aviv school, said that "a journey to Poland is a journey to the Holocaust. We don't visit other sites, except for Jewish sites. We are not tourists, but pilgrims." "We go there seeking our ancestors," Asaf commented before his group in one of the meetings, "I still remember the first crying, pupils caressing each other, a strong feeling of togetherness, of being one." "We did undergo some preparations in regard to the Polish culture, but very little," said Yona, an ex-delegate, "our journey was very much focused on Jewish sites. You can call it a pilgrimage, or you can say it is due to the time restrictions. We were actually running from camp to camp. Nine camps in eight days, don't you think it's a lot?"

Preparations focused on Jewish heritage, Jewish learning in the various *Batei-Midrash* (religious high schools) of Poland, and important religious texts composed there. The format and contents of the texts which accompanied the preparations were respectively very different. These were primarily composed of selected pages from religious works written by Jews in Poland.

Reading the Holocaust

Holocaust delegations are now a taken-for-granted part of Israeli educational reality. Dozens of delegations are formed each year. Each of these delegations sees its journey as embodying a unique and incomparable experience. Reading the Holocaust through the eyes of these delegations and their handbooks offers a unique window into the dynamics of social commemoration and social amnesia. It illustrates the instability of collective memory: one's memory is one's amnesia— Jewish history, for example, is commemorated by religious schools but is missing from secular kibbutzim youth movements.

Summing up, it appears that although local schools are always somewhat different, there is a strong inter-group similarity, derived from the school's affiliation with a certain educational stream, such as the state-secular, state-religious, or kibbutz education. Current preparations and journey handbooks are to a large extent recycled from previous materials. There is a cultural transmission within each educational stream. In kibbutzim's schools, the "Jewish" and "Israeli" focus is replaced by a detailed description of Poland's general history. However, this so-called universal representation in fact follows the kibbutz's local interest in topics such as socialism, solidarity and industrialization. In the case of Hashomer Hatzair, the kibbutz youth movement, one sees an overemphasis on ghetto uprisings. However, this is not an extreme case of the Zionist focus on "heroism." The uprisings, in the preparations and handbooks of Hashomer Hatzair, are not directly contrasted with the "lamb to slaughter" Holocaust Jew (although this comparison is in the background, to be sure). Uprisings are rather appropriated as belonging to the legacy of the youth movement. Their image and cause are glorified and idealized. There is no reference to the conflicting aspects of an a priori lost rebel, an issue which is gradually appearing in the ministry's Holocaust textbooks.

State-religious schools, in contrast, appropriate the Holocaust as belonging to the Jewish realm of "lost heritage," a heritage which was rekindled in religious Israel. The Holocaust is thus seen as a bridge to

Jewish history and a locus of Jewish solidarity. Finally, state-secular schools view the Holocaust as a lever to consolidate an Israeli identity, namely the self-identification with a sovereign and strong Israeli state. This view positions the Holocaust as a point of departure from Jewish history, a culmination of the diaspora from which Israel has broken away and dissociated itself. It opposes the Holocaust Jew to the "new Israeli." In recent years, however, this trend has been contested by new ministers of education coming from more liberal parties. Amnon Rubinstein, the current minister of education, recently said in a radio program that he is determined to change two things about the delegations: "first, emphasizing the loss of democratic principles before the Holocaust. Second, the fact that not only Jews were victimized during the Holocaust. Notwithstanding this, we keep the focus on the genocide of the Jewish people. This is a complex picture, but we have intelligent pupils" (interviewed in *Raz* 1995). The new minister's views no doubt also find expression in the ministry's course program.

The claim that the Holocaust is a key symbol in Israeli identity construction is more often made than substantiated. Perhaps it is of no surprise that different educational streams make use of a different narrative in regard to the Holocaust. Perhaps it is also of no surprise that Israelis would view the Holocaust as something which happened primarily to Jews. This study provides a detailed ideological reading of three competing narratives of the Holocaust. These narratives, or worldviews, will arguably continue to play a dominant role in contemporary Israeli society. The study also described the gap between the ministry's course rationale and the actual nationalistic narrative inculcated in the state-secular schools, which are supposed to be directly influenced by the ministry. This gap serves as evidence to the general sociological contention that educational frames are inherently a negotiated order.

Afterword: The Holocaust as Simulation

The social research regarding the perceptions of the Holocaust in Israel has been focused on the real ramifications of the Holocaust—be they the reactions of second and third generations or historical studies into what the pre-state Jewish leaders did (or did not) do in order to help the survivors. There is very little, if any, research that studies the Holocaust today as *simulation.* The very idea of the Holocaust as simulation sounds absurd and indeed antagonistic, particularly as it appears to echo the infamous surge of "Holocaust denial." But saying that the Holocaust is now perceived as simulation has nothing to do with denying that it indeed took place. On the contrary, I wish to argue that we are in an accelerated process of moving from the "real history" to the representation of the Holocaust by other means. As survivors naturally pass away, we are moving from first-hand recollections to second- and third-hand representations. The Holocaust is therefore entering—for better or worse—the realm of the simulated.

Recently two major Holocaust memorials—Yad Vashem and the U.S. Holocaust Museum in Washington, D.C.—have opened a home-page on the internet, where one can "surf" into a virtual world dedicated to the Holocaust. As could be expected, the simulation is replete with denotations of real ideology. The most striking ideological difference concerns the ethnic representation of the Holocaust. "Yad Vashem," opens its homepage, "is the Holocaust memorial of the Jewish people.... At the core of the Holocaust was the decision to kill the Jews—six millions of whom were murdered." The U.S. Holocaust Memorial Museum, in contrast, opens its homepage by telling the readers about its most recent activity—"an ecumenical gathering for the dead and the suffering in the former Yugoslavia...[where] seven religious leaders offered readings and called America's attention to the 'ethnic cleansing' in the former Yugoslavia." Following is a long self-presentation of the museum. The word "Jew" or one of its derivatives, however, does not appear in it even once.

The study of the Holocaust as simulation acknowledges its ideological shaping and representation. Rather than asking what is represented, we should ask how the Holocaust is represented, by and for whom, and for what purposes. The simulated Holocaust is an a priori politicized Holocaust. Israeli society today knowingly fosters a dialectical relationship with the Holocaust. When "the world" is concerned, Israeli society embraces the Holocaust, insisting on the exclusive association it has with it. Notable foreign visitors to Israel are thus always brought to Yad Vashem, and are publicly condemned if they refuse to do so. Or consider, for an opposite example, Israel's refusal to formally participate in the *European* ceremony held in Auschwitz to mark fifty years of the camp's "liberation." When, however, the Holocaust is considered within Israeli society, it is subject to several competing interpretations, three of which have been detailed here. The co-existence of these contrasting interpretation is made possible because of the use of simulations.

"Surfing the Holocaust" serves to invoke a picture of varied Holocaust surfaces and facades (homepages) that are now readily available through a click on the mouse or one's school of choice. The Holocaust is already part of the marketplace, a *"shoa'a*-business" that we have become used to consuming as TV watchers and cinema-goers. There are currently packaged tours of the U.S. east coast, offered to Israelis, that begin in the Holocaust museum and finish in Disney World: a true journey between simulations. These simulations are evidently aimed in particular toward the youth. When marketed as pedagogic program, for example as part of the Holocaust tours, these simulations also illustrate the usurpation of youth culture by middle-age society.

During the Gulf War, when Israel passively faced the threat of gas-armed Iraqi missiles, the image of the Holocaust resurfaced again from the national Pandora's box of anxieties. For one of Israel's foremost historians, Emmanuel Sivan, this signified the *weakness* of Israeli collective memory. Why, asked Sivan,[5] did Israelis retreated to the Holocaust rather than to their own experience of difficult wars, especially the 1948 War, where twelve hundred citizens, among them 190 children under the age of 14, were killed? According to Sivan, forgetting 1948 and retreating to the Holocaust as a national womb was a symptom of weakness.

Sivan's article is directly connected to Elkana's request—with which this chapter opens—that Israel forget the Holocaust. Sivan, it seems, offers a historical solution to Elkana's problem, pointing to the 1948 War as a "natural" framework for a "genuine" collective memory that could replace the "fictive myth" of the Holocaust. At the same time, however, Sivan also admits to the futility of this attempt. It was the Holocaust, after all, that surfaced during the Gulf War, and not the 1948 siege on Jerusalem. Moreover, Sivan's "solution" is just as programmatic and biased. It also pinpoints the particular experience of the Gulf War in Israel. Wars, in general, hinge on and summon a tribal "we-feeling." It is in such instances that the contours of collective memory resurface most blatantly. These assertions take us into the realm of the Gulf War, which is the subject of the next chapter.

NOTES

1. Yehuda Elkana, Ha'aretz daily newspaper, 2.3.1988, p. 13.
2. This chapter is based on research funded by the Israel Foundation Trustees (Ford Foundation) under the title "The Construction of Collective Memory and National Identity in the Context of Israeli Youth Delegations to Concentration Camps," Grant 94 (1994–96).
3. The Israeli system of education has its early roots in the pre-state period, at which time it was comprised of ideologically and politically affiliated streams. These streams later became different wings in the Ministry of Education, titled as "state-secular," "state-religious," and "settlement education" (kibbutzim and moshavim). Each stream has largely kept its unique curriculum and extracurricular activities, as well as textbooks and teaching methods (see also Kleinberger 1969).
4. "The righteous amongst the nations" is an Israeli idiom designating non-Jews who risked their lives to help the persecuted Jews in the Holocaust.
5. Immanuel Sivan, "Familiar, but Strange," Ha'arretz 8.2.91 p. 15.

3. SERIALIZING WAR
The Interrupted Discourse

$\textit{A}$ few months after the Gulf War, two videocassettes were released by the marketing division of the Israeli National Television. One was a collection of authentic sights and sounds from the war, while the other was comprised of an anthology of Gulf War excerpts taken from a popular TV satire named "This Is It." The sales of the second cassette far exceeded those of the first, and many even purchased it to send to relatives abroad. It was hence not the authentic collection of news and reports, but rather the satire which was culturally chosen to stand as a testimony of the Gulf War.

The first question that comes to mind is why was the "real thing"— all packed with sounds of sirens, dazzling sights of bombing Baghdad, areas hit in Israel by missiles, and gas-masked Israelis—largely ignored, whereas a take off comical representation of the same situation gained enormous popularity? The off-the-cuff answer would obviously be that Israelis prefer to forget a battlefield in which they were only passive victims. This explanation may well apply to the failure of the first product, but by no means accounts for the success of the second. Indeed, the vast popularity which characterized the broadcasts of "This Is It" during the Gulf War, eventually transforming it into part of the collective memory related to that event, warrants an explanation in its own right.

The question of appropriating a comical text into the Israeli collective memory is rendered more intriguing by two additional facts. One, such a comical addition to the national scrapbook seems out of place, if not diametrically opposed to the cannon of hallowed nation-building myths. Two, this contrast is further sharpened by the program's sarcastic zeal to deconstruct those myths of origin. If Israeli identity hinges on collectivism and 'straight talk' realism (Katriel 1986, 1991) then such wry devices of tongue-in-cheek and parody could not be admitted into the canonized treasure of national memorabilia. However, not only was the product a best seller, but the actors appearing on the show have become identified with the characters they played and enjoy a status of national celebrities. Key phrases from the show have been constantly quoted both in the media and in everyday life, and there was even a suggestion to award the creators of the program the most elevated national award—the "Israel Prize."

The media narrative in question was successful because it offered an articulated form of indelible forgetfulness. "Forget the Gulf War!" was the subtext of "This Is It," whose show offered a way of transforming an intolerable experience into a non-representational narrative of a different order. In the following sections I analyze how "This Is It" operated as a self-contained, interpretative simulation that could enter the cultural vacuum of the Gulf War. But first let me elaborate on the social meaning of the Gulf War as experienced in Israel.

Israel in the Gulf War

The Gulf War (officially January to March 1991) spelled a new kind of military experience for Israel (see also Shaham and Ra'anan 1991; Werman 1993). It did not entail the mobilization of forces, army reserves etc., but rather the demobilization of Israeli society, which that was put into the sealed room and waited there for instructions—a passive and previously unfamiliar situation. The Gulf War was later known as the war that turned "the rear into the front"; meaning that the country itself and its civilian population became the battleground on which Saddam Hussein's missiles could and did land.

A few weeks before Operation Desert Storm commenced, many Israelis deserted their homes and fled either abroad or to places inside the country marked by experts as being out of Saddam's SCUD (ground-to-ground) missiles' range. That was despite continuous attempts by military pundits to allay fears and to reassure the public that Saddam was very unlikely to strike at Israeli civilian targets, for his knowledge of Israeli military deterrents would prevent him from considering it. Even if such a remote eventuality occurred, maintained politicians as well as commentators, the Israeli war machine would know how to put an immediate stop to it. The first strike would be also the last.

The euphoric feeling of an instant victory which was transmitted by the world media to Israeli homes amplified the shock of the first missile attack. Israelis were caught by surprise in the middle of the night and rushed to their designated sealed rooms frantically trying to complete the insulation procedures and to put the gas masks on. A number of panic-stricken persons died of suffocation caused by not removing the filter caps of the masks. Confusion and uncertainty were total. TV and radio were for a few hours unable to provide any information, give guidance or offer comfort. Telephone switchboards became overloaded and lines were out of order. Foreign broadcasting stations such as the BBC World Service reported a possible chemical attack and no military or political communiqués were issued. Further attacks and their resulting devastation coupled with the indecisive and presumably undecided response of the Israeli political and military establishment, confirmed that the situation was out of control.

A new, improvised order of daily routine had begun. Most people did not go to work for a few weeks, outings were limited to shopping, and urgent errands were made with gas mask boxes dangling from shoulders (Danet, Loshitzky and Bechar-Israeli 1993). Schools were closed and home became both a total sanctuary and an information center (Ben-David and Lavee 1992). Radio stations merged into one channel and TV broadcast 24 hours a day. The country was divided into graded zones of safety and people moved to relatives and hotels seeking refuge from their own unsafe residence. Tel-Aviv, considered a high-risk zone, was deserted by many of its inhabitants. Jerusalem, previously seldom visited for fear of terrorism, was now considered a most unlikely target for missile attacks and became a safe haven for thousands of refugees, as they were called in the media. Those refugees were indeed subject to public condemnation by politicians and others (most notably, the mayor of Tel-Aviv). The popular war sticker was "I stayed in Tel-Aviv."[1]

For many Israelis (arguably of Ashkenazi origin) the Gulf War experience was a reminder of the Holocaust. In an article entitled "Reflections on the Gulf War," a famous Israeli psychiatrist analyzed that:

> This war has changed everything. Instead of being conducted somewhere in the front lines, your city and your home became the front. You are stuck in your own home and you must wait, wait…. Suddenly you recall experiences

you have long managed to forget, experiences belonging to our personal and collective past in Europe in the 40's. (Stern 1992:53)

Similar feelings are conveyed in the following excerpt taken from the curator's forward to the catalog of "Real Time: Graphic Texts of the Gulf War," an exhibition held in the Tel-Aviv Museum after the war:

> The Gulf War elicited in Israel a sense of helplessness, passivity and impotence of an attacked country being threatened with mass destruction and yet unable to take an active part in its self-defense. This situation was associated, in the collective memory, with the period of Jewish diaspora. (Doner 1991:1)

The feelings of impotence had been later associated more directly with Israeli men. As Yuchtman-Yaar, Peres and Goldberg observed,

> Israel's passivity in the Gulf War was especially frustrating to the male reservists who, instead of being called for active military duties, found themselves waiting in sealed rooms together with their families, having little to do except for complaining about their ill-fate as unused fighters. (1994:7)

Forgetting its national impotence has thus become a unifying force for the sealed Israeli society. Symbolically, the instant hero of the Gulf War was not a soldier but an anonymous citizen who, after his home was destroyed by a direct SCUD hit, hoisted the Israeli flag on top of the ruins. He and his flag became quoted and glorified overnight, and the symbolic act was televised and shown repeatedly in the news. Consequently, politicians and others called the people to "wave up their flags." Habima, Tel-Aviv's national theatre, was wrapped with a huge flag, "as if it were a coffin" (Doner 1991:5).

The implications of the Gulf War for Israeli society therefore included, primarily, a loss of faith in the military and the political leadership, a loss of the illusion of national independence (being subject to American interests and prescriptions), as well as a novel form of family life characterized by loss of former role differentiation and a forced togetherness. It is therefore not far-fetched to argue that the Gulf War paved the way for the Israeli-Palestinian peace process.

Framing the Text

"This Is It," screened every day during the Gulf War, was not a new show for the Israeli T.V. viewer. In fact, its weekly presentation had enjoyed a longstanding record of high-rate viewing and a growing circle of fans. It was originally a youth show, designed and written for the "teen" age-group with interwoven reports on the rock and pop scene, short quizzes, a film guide and clips of popular music. Most of the fifty minutes of "This Is It" were devoted to the sketches played by the house-cast whose dramatic reputation was recognized outside the show in the theater and other media appearances. The contents often consisted of critical commentary of Israeli life from state affairs and the way they are handled by the government, to a parody on habits, styles and antics of Israeli culture. Thus, for example, the satirical scrutiny of the show made fun of the passion of many Israelis for gatherings of communal sing-alongs and threw into relief latent fascist elements ingrained in it. The satirical gaze of the show was often also directed to other, "dignified" television programs. "This Is It," like "Saturday Night Live," "SCTV" and other satires, was hence based on a self-reflexive, intertextual and deconstructive narrative (Olson 1987). It reflected on the medium of television in general, on other popular shows and particular genres of television, sometimes even on its own texture. All of these characteristics, already well-known to the program's audience, were intensified during the Gulf War.

The collection cassette of "This Is It" consisted of six episodes, six variations of the same critical theme. The first episode dealt with the temporary merger between the various media channels during the war—one radio, one television, and military spokesmen working together with civilians—as a wrestling match where the interlocked contestants are forced to appear as one body while fighting to the hilt. The purpose of that merger—providing exact and real-time information—was scorned by portraying that information was, in fact, totally ambiguous and delivered in a mixture of euphoric relaxation and hysterical panic. The spokesman for the Israeli army (named "General Marshmallow") was presented as ignorant of the facts which literally hit him in the face while he is doing his best to deny them. While producing calming and reassuring messages to the interviewers, he is being exposed to a missile attack that destroys all the toy model weapons he displays to demonstrate the might of the Israeli army.

In the second episode, apologetic Israelis were shown as they fled their homes to seek refuge in either Eilat—a remote, safe, seaside resort—or abroad. In either case, the fugitive explained away their escape by resorting to old Zionist clichés such as "We are relieving the burden from the prime minister who now has to care for one less citizen," or "Everywhere is Israel." The blatant absurdity of the pretexts offered by the "inter-viewees" reinforced the message that the gulf between the myth of "strong Israel" and the reality of SCUDs does not allow for any form of symbolic reconciliation, and that the only resolution to that crisis is running away from it. This very solution was also adopted by the media agent—the interviewer, who joined the refugees on their flight out of Tel-Aviv.

The realization that words can no longer furnish symbolic identifi-cation with the collectivity took the form of discrediting prophetic wis-dom to the extreme in the third episode. A figure highly reminiscent of a widely respected, though controversial, Moroccan saint (called the Baba Buba—a direct allusion to the *Baba Sali*),[2] was enacted as an authority of which the media took heed. The twisted and nonsensical interpretations he produced constituted a combination between out-right ignorance, sheer stupidity and undeniable feeble-mindedness. Yet for the lack of other sources of knowledge, the public treated his words with credibility particularly as they are intent on offering some prepos-terous linguistic solace to the dilemma of identification with the col-lectivity while deserting it. It should be noted that the presentation of a much revered Oriental rabbi as a laughing stock fell short of trans-gressing one of the most guarded taboos in Israeli culture—that of overt ethnic disrespect (for the importance of such sacred men in pop-ular Israeli culture, see Bilu and Ben Ari 1992). Evidently that was another testimony to the collapse of symbolic codes at that time. The fact that the cassette retained two sketches concerning that figure could either mean that the disintegration of the cultural system survived the war period and persisted in Israeli society afterwards, or that the cas-sette did not bear any representational reflection regarding everyday reality. However, the figure of the Baba—the Oriental rabbi—quickly disappeared from the sketches of "This Is It" once the war was over.

The fourth episode paid a visit to the civil defense units, which were shown to be in total disarray as they raised the alarm in the wrong areas and entered a state of panic when the sirens were sounded by them-selves. The personnel was depicted as being engaged in constant bick-ering over their areas of jurisdiction while from within the rubble and havoc caused by the SCUDs emerge looters who, under the eyes of the internally embittered law, take their plunder away. The political system was also presented as indecisive as one politician declared "There is a limit to our forbearance"; whereas another stated that "We shall decide when and where to react."

The fifth episode contained a sketch showing a head full of lice facing extermination by a new chemical agent—an anti-lice shampoo. Realizing their impending unavoidable fate, the lice decide to look for another head to settle on. The association between the Holocaust and the broken pledge of Israeli society to avert any possibility of it happening again was only too obvious and so was the inevitable conclusion, which in no uncertain terms was against the grain of Zionist ideology. The sixth and last episode depicted family life as an area where the assumed structure in conjugal relationships is reversed. The women are strong and their husbands are hopelessly nervous and anxious to the extent of malfunctioning. "My daddy prays to the army spokesman" says a child and another adds that since both his parents are home, no one knows how to behave anymore. On a visit to the video library a frightened husband refuses to borrow any film which contains the slightest suggestion of threat, to the extent that even *Heidi of the Mountains* is disqualified on the grounds that no-one can stroll the mountains not equipped with a gas mask. The offer of Mel Brooks' "The Mad History of the World" is turned down because "we see it all the time on CNN."

Another sketch focusing on inverted relationship featured a ventriloquist and his animated doll. The doll, which recognizes its master's inability to control it, rebels against his reluctance to leave the sealed room to which they are both confined. It takes command and leads the master-turned-doll out. The subject becomes an object and the object is transformed into a subject. Hence only by a complete disavowal of will and self can the master be rescued from the fate of fear and nothingness.

A Poetics of Reversal

The "This Is It" narrative offered a way of transcending the war zone into an acontextual realm of "reversed order" where antitheticals can be thrown into satirical relief. Escaping reality demanded that the very possibility of a realist narrative would be eliminated. The notion of the realist narrative has been articulated in a number of studies (e.g., Heath 1981; Hebdige and Hurd 1978; MacCabe 1985; Morley 1980; Stevens 1978). It can be summarized with three major points. First, the dominant mode of narration is based upon a plot construction that favors linearity and motivational credibility. This is deconstructed in the case of "This Is It" through the use of circular, self-referential independent episodes, in which the protagonists' actions are not informed by their motives (as in the inability to produce credible information, or even to select a videocassette for home viewing). Second, realistic narrativity is emphasized and made transparent through the masking of the formal properties of the medium. In the case of "This Is it," participants were often led to on-the-spot improvisation, accompanied by restrained laughter at what they were acting while they were acting it. This feature of circumstances was unavoidably retained in the recordings on the cassette, thus endowing it with narrative positions of reflexivity and self-awareness very much like in the distancing literary stance of a third person narrator. Third, along with a tendency to structure the narrative from an omniscient point of view, the realist text works to place spectators in such a position that they will identify with the shifting points of view of the characters within the narrative. In the case of "This Is It," the "authority" of the narrator (as well as of the news commentator, the reporter and the army spokesman) was mocked and obliterated, and the spectators were made to identify with either the camera (as they watch the anticipated failures of the characters) or brought to reflect upon their own situation.

Linearity and motivational credibility—both dominant signs and prerequisites of the realist text—were also underpinned in "This Is It" by the introduction of cultural archetypes: not only the acknowledged Oriental rabbi, but also elderly and children characters. Six elderly characters—three men and three women—were presented as vicarious commentators on the situation. All six were shown to demonstrate a haven of sanity at the midst of cultural upheaval. However, the men projected an entirely different image. They assimilated the war experience into their own private realm and treated the absurdity of the situation as part of normal life. They indulged in fantasies of eliminating Saddam just like the press of the day. They also discussed with unshaken serenity the ineffectual conduct of the military and attributed the disruption of daily life by the war to their normal mistrust of the world. National havoc and disarray were discussed as part and parcel of the confused and uncertain routine of the elderly. The liminal, suspended time of the war situation was deemed compatible with the state of being old, which could be considered as being out of culture and out of time (Hazan 1980, 1994). The elderly women, however, while also projecting an acultural condition, did not display confusion and fantasy, but an adherence to mundane existence of cooking and mending clothes. They even discussed Saddam Hussein's sex appeal as a "tall, tanned, handsome man" who could replace their own men who are "out of commission." Their acontextual position enabled them to offer historically reflexive views comparing past to present, such as the statement that "once a war was a war, men would go to the army, men used to be men, nowadays every man is a Schwartzkopf."

Another island of sanity was presented by children, who were portrayed as continuing their lifestyle undisturbed by the situation. Unlike the elderly, however, they were not shown to be guided by fantasy or nature, but by play. Their sandpit existence was depicted as an observation point from which the insane adult world could be viewed from the perspective of a game unaffected by reality.

The narrative of "This Is It" therefore hinged on circular, rather than linear, time. It offered a reversed order where men of power (spokesmen, politicians, adults) were mocked while marginal characters (Orientals, elderly and children) were depicted as sources of mythical wisdom—wisdom which is not based on the here and now of military intelligence or political negotiations. Another example of circularity—both temporal and compositional—was provided in a carnival-like party where all the participants in the sketches gathered to deliver a song framing the war within Jewish mythology as yet another link in a never-ending chain of intermittent torments and redemption. Ceasefire was declared on a date that coincided with the Jewish festival of Purim—a day celebrating the salvation of the Jews at the time of Esther from the evil intention of *Haman* to exterminate them. Jewish tradition designated Purim as a festival of masquerades and social reversals and "This Is It," inspired by that spirit, presented a two-pronged ahistorical tale of salvation. On the one hand, there was the presentation of the whole event of the war as not real, but a festival of masks—gas masks. On the other hand, it was versed as one scene in the perennial plot of Jewish survival—an "eternal return" with the same villains, only with different names and places—not unlike the modern serialized TV drama. This routine of torture and revival precludes the war from being a unique event and incorporates it into an ahistorical time of no chronological order.

Non-representational narratives, as stated before, deconstruct the formal properties of the medium (Waugh 1984). A prominent strategy for doing this is metacommunication. "This Is It" thus highlighted the inability of broadcasters and journalists to construct a cogent story composed of a string of coherent images. Indeed, this failure in communication became the governing concern of the cassette, rather than the "real" event—the war. The Gulf War was constituted as a "media event." First, it was an event that was media dependent and media generated. As one of the elderly commentators explained, "If we burn Saddam's oil wells there will be no electricity for power stations and with no electricity there will be no television and with no television there will be no war." Second, it was a media event which justified itself as such and derived its existence and strength from that fact. As one of the elderly women answered an inquiry for directions to the repeat broadcast made by the interviewer, she instructs him to "go straight, left and right and there you will find your own self." The only recognized reality is that of the media which accommodates the collectivity, the self and the capacity to reflect upon all these. In other words, it is a self-contained, self-sufficient non-representational media narrative.

The message that This is Media and Nothing Else was transfixed to the postwar context of daily consumerism as one of the This Is It cassette marketable properties. The cassette was distributed in most stationery stores and book shops, thus becoming both a recreational product and an item of nostalgia and war memorabilia. At the beginning of the tape there appeared a video advertisement for other program-based cassettes produced and sold by the marketing department of the Educational Television. Hence the "This Is It in the Gulf," as the cassette was entitled, was introduced as an item on one shelf with other likewise products such as cassettes teaching reading comprehension, Hebrew grammar, mathematics, English, preschool education and family therapy. This banalization of the void of collapsing codes was thus allied to an array of items of socialization and crisis management, rendering it, by virtue of its framing, an educational device.

The evident fact that life returned to "normal" after the war also meant a partial restoration of public trust in the authorities and a reconfirmation of the previously collapsed cultural codes. Israelis went about their daily affairs as if nothing in their existential world had been shattered. The cassette, therefore, while being self-presented as a media narrative about the media, excluded from its contents elements which could have brought the simulation back to its original ground and defy the metacommunicative message. Two sketches that were broadcast during the war were editorially expurgated from the product. These two sketches presented life-threatening situations unmediated by the transformative mechanism of turning them into media-centered events. The first was a sketch showing the distribution posts for gas masks run by the army dishing out antiquated faulty masks of evident uselessness. The other showed Saddam's doubles and look-alikes that could not be distinguished from the authentic figure, with the message being that since there is no way of identifying the original there is also no way of destroying it. The invocation of the indestructible vampire or the werewolf was obvious. Both sketches were poignant reminders of a situation which still existed, and their removal spelt the need to avoid that situation.

Global Responses to the Gulf War

Israel's experience of the Gulf War was unique. In the West, particularly in France and the U.S., leftist intellectuals publicly questioned the reality and necessity of the war. For Israel, in contrast, the war was undeniably real and the coalition forces were the only shield between Tel-Aviv and the Iraqi SCUDs. For Western intellectuals, the Gulf War was a remote occurrence, a "media event" to be analyzed and gaze at; for the Israeli collectivity that suffered the attacks—intellectuals included—the encounter with war was close, literally at home, and with personal psychological ramifications.

To understand the gulf between Western and Israeli conceptions of the war, let me introduce two Western intellectual voices: Jean Baudrillard and Noam Chomsky. Baudrillard argued that the Gulf War did not, literally, "take place" (*n'a pas eu lieu;* see Baudrillard 1991). It existed, for its audience as well as its American generals, on TV screens and through CNN reports. The Gulf War brought to extreme the substitution of reality by media-projected simulacra. This all-embracing substitution constitutes what Baudrillard terms "hyper-reality."

> In the Gulf War, which replaced the soldier with the hostage as its main protagonist, we also—as audience—were held hostages by the global media, depending on it for more information, by which we are bombarded through the screen.... We have created a gigantic apparatus of simulation enabling us to reproduce the act "in vitro." Instead of the catastrophe of the real, we prefer the exile of the virtual, of which television is the universal mirror. (Baudrillard 1991:11–16)

The Gulf War did not take place, argues Baudrillard (*"ceci n'est pas une guerre,"* he writes, alluding to Megritte) because it was not maintained as a reciprocal act between two enemies. "In the Gulf War, the enemy was but a stranger, a code name on the computer's monitor, while the war was a-sexual, surgical, launched from afar, viewed at a distance ... war-processing" (1991: 63, 64). This is intriguingly similar to Chomsky's question, raised in regard to Operation Desert Storm. "What War?" he asks, and replies: "As I understand the concept 'War,' it involves two sides in combat, say, shooting at each other. This did not happen in the Gulf" (1992:51).[3] The Gulf War, according to Baudrillard, was sustained as a war against "the Other."

For Saddam, it was a war against the unknown (*L'Inconnu*), against the American super-technology and the super-powers of the coalition.... For him, war constituted an act of magical provocation, after which the rest is in God's (or the Arab masses) hands.... For the Americans, Saddam was an abstraction—they do not understand him. Nothing personal. They are not interested in the game of power he wants to play; they will demolish him in their own time. They are fighting against its otherness (*alterité*) in an attempt to reduce this otherness, convert it, or annihilate it if it is irreducible (as in the case of the Indians). (1991: 30, 31)

Finally, claims Baudrillard, "the Israelis, they do not share the Americans' excitement towards the war. They view the Other in its nude, without illusion nor hesitation. The Other, the Arab, is unconvertible, his otherness beyond change, does not need to be changed, it has to be annihilated" (p. 31).[4]

While "This Is It" offered a Baudrillardian view of the Gulf War, it could only do so in the guise of satire. At the end of each of its subversive statements, "This Is It" asks "can you hear me laughing?" Baudrillard was speaking of the war, of a hyper-reality that consumed our senses. "This Is It" was escaping the war, speaking to the Israelis' need to forget its reality. "This Is It" was the "real" simulacra, not the war. As McGuigan (1992:249) aptly remarks, "although Baudrillard's deliberately ironic conceit illuminates the processes of 'media war,' the casualties of 'incontinent ordinances' and 'carpet bombing' may not have appreciated his wit."

However, Baudrillard is also partly right. The consequences of the Gulf War for Israeli society were not so much the result of the occurrences in Kuwait, neither of the few SCUD missiles that were launched by Iraq. Above all, the effect of the Gulf War was constituted through its electronically mediated simulacra. It was seen through CNN, explained through radio and television, experienced through the media. The new script of impotence dictated by that war, as well as the interpretative havoc it evoked, were both created and reproduced through the media. It was hence first and foremost the media which made the Gulf War such a lasting experience for Israeli citizens, as well as for the world (see the recent literature on the Gulf War as the first true "televised war," e.g., Jowett 1993; Kellner 1992; MacArthur 1992; Mowlana et al. 1992; Taylor 1992). "The war's relatively short duration," argues Jowett, "meant that events could be seen in their gruesome entirety, unfolding like a super-lengthy Bernardo Bertolucci movie epic, where the audience keep coming back night after night to see the next episode" (1993:63).

Local Responses: The Interrupted System

The local response to the Gulf War should now be read again in the context of Israel's military history, this time connecting it to the discourse on collectivism and collective memory. Kimmerling has offered to conceptualize Israel's continued involvement in wars as an "interrupted system," which is

> a social system in the rare situation of a sudden but temporary interruption of many social processes. [In the face of war] the system changes from one faced with many goals that generally conflict with each other—as in every open and modern society—to a system having only two main goals. Most of the social resources (manpower and material) are mobilized (to the front). The second and complementary goal is to "maintain" the system so that it will be able to return to its previous state as quickly and inexpensively as possible. (1985:3)

The interruption is a fact of life and has to be accommodated as seriously as possible, since war is perceived as threatening both the physical and socio-political existence of the collectivity as a whole. Defeat in war would not only mean a loss of prestige or territory or a blow to national interests, but the total annihilation of Israeli society. The dominance of the warfare situation has shaped the face of Israeli society. For one example, it largely replaced social stratification with a new and significant reference group: the Israeli Defense Force (IDF). Wars became instruments for collective enlistment and the army became the dominant vehicle for social stratification.

The Gulf War broke the spell of this magic circle of "interruptions" and the way it previously dictated Israeli life. In the Gulf War, there was an interruption but no mobilization of forces; a call to collectivism without a real "we-feeling." The satire of "This Is It" is the best illustration of that cultural vacuum. Being a real war without the dynamics of such, the Gulf War threw into relief the disguises of the Israeli collectivity, its rhetorical ritual of tribal solidarity. The Gulf War introduced Israel into the global "risk society" (Beck 1992), where "political conflicts are increasingly defined by the distributions of 'bads'—hazards and risks" (Lash and Urry 1994:33). This is a shift from the centrality of the nation-state into a global awareness of ecological hazards such as Chernobyl, the ozone layer, Brazilian rain forests, and the Gulf War.

The most important point in which the Gulf War experience and "This Is It" converge is where there is no higher authority with which to identify. The Israeli military, the previous stronghold of collectivism, was demobilized. The Israeli government was perceived as blindly following the directives of the Bush administration. And the coalition forces were perceived as incompetent, since they failed in both preventing the SCUD attacks and in capturing Saddam. The inability to identify is brought into comic peaks in "This Is It." Again, it does so by diverting from the conventions of the realist text. One of the realist narrative's sources of power is its ability to situate the viewer as the subject.[5] That is to say, the viewer is seduced into unconscious identification with the narrative figures. The viewer "sees" what is shown as "real" to him or her by means of unconscious identifications, unconscious projections, introjections and displacements by the viewer himself or herself in relationship to the images screened. This could be done, in the case of the Gulf War, through identifying with the "good guys" (the Americans, especially General Schwartzkopf) and demonizing the "bad guys" (the Iraqis). This was, indeed, the strategy of all realist representations, whether intensified by propaganda or not. In contrast, I have argued throughout this chapter that the "This Is It" show did just the opposite—namely situated its viewer as the object. It evoked self-awareness rather than typifications of the Other. It demystified and mocked rather than subscribed to the "realist" media reproductions of hegemonic (American) ideology.

Afterword: The Gulf War as Simulation

It is easy to see why I used the concept of the simulation for the analysis of "This Is It." Self-reflexive, intertextual and deconstructive, "This Is It" reflected on the reality of the Gulf War as well as on the medium of television in general, on other popular shows, even on its own texture.

All of these characteristics, already well-known to the program's audience, were intensified during the Gulf War. "This Is It" used simulation in order to replace the "real" Gulf War.

"This Is It" was more successful than the realistic videocassette because of two complementary reasons. First, it denied the realistic narrative of the Gulf War, refraining from direct reevocation of that unfavorable war experience. Instead, it reflected on that experience through a satirical, deconstructive gaze of self-awareness. Moreover, it also provided its viewers with a constructive, myth-like script of alternative reality. It hence employed two diametrically opposed narrative devices. On the one hand, satire: a representational, linear, object-evoking device. On the other hand, myth: a non-representational, cyclical, subject-constructing device.

The first narrative could mock the daily havoc of Israel during the Gulf War—the useless gas masks, the irresponsible sirens, the uncooperative media union. The second narrative, in contrast, could employ cultural archetypes in order to evoke the traditional notion of "the wars of the Jews," the Jewish people as attacked and besieged throughout its historical existence. It was the combined workings of these two narratives that made "This Is It" so successful.

"This Is It," both during the Gulf War and before, was a show intended for youth. As such, it has always been satirical, biting the establishment in its sensitive spots. The combination of satire and collectivism that characterized "This Is It," however, can be analyzed as yet another usurpation of youth culture by middle-age society. Being a youthful satire, This Is It could have taken its criticism to the edge, and stopped there; but it went further. The critical scrutiny of the satire culminated in the legitimation of the social order. This is why This Is It also connected the experience of the Gulf War to the mythical narrative of Jewish passivity in the diaspora.

Being a youth TV show, "This Is It" was, in the final analysis, seen as harmless and innocent. It was a simulation, not "reality." It provided a distance from which the Gulf War could be safely gazed at, without committing to realist representations or to their derived questions, disarray, and criticism. Was Israel correct in obeying the U.S. and refraining from retaliating against the Iraqi missile attacks? Were the coalition forces really victorious (but then why is Saddam still on his throne)? These provocative questions were hidden away by the well-wishing, laughable comedy. This non-committing quality of the simulation is also found at the heart of the "dispirited rebellion" of youth in Israel, which is the subject of the following chapter.

NOTES

1. However, when huge signposts with the collectivist-patriotic war slogan "I stayed in Tel Aviv" were erected in the city, an invisible hand added to it the word freier (i.e., 'sucker'), so that the result looked like: "I (freier) stayed in Tel Aviv."

2. The mocking representation of the Oriental rabbi in "This Is It" did not result in any public protest against ethnic disrespect. This could have been due to the fact that as a satirical show, "This Is It" was actually expected to make fun of such phenomena; it would have been foolish to criticize a satire for being disrespectful.

3. Chomsky is speaking here against the use of propaganda in American media during the Gulf War—"the remarkable control of American consciousness during and after the war" (Schiller 1992:23) by the Bush administration's Gulf War policies.

4. This generalized interpretation of Baudrillard obviously did not, and could not, foresee the recent developments in the peace process between Israel and the PLO.

5. This notion was developed by the "1970s film theory," articulated mainly through the Society for Education in Film and Television's Journal Screen, with regard to Hollywood films: see, for example, de Lauretis (1984); Doane (1987); Kuhn (1982); Metz (1977); Mulvay (1975); Penley (1989); Silverman (1988).

4. TAMING YOUTH CULTURE
The Generational Discourse

*I*n recent years, the intergenerational conflict in Israel has been expressed mainly through the idea of "abolishing the collective." In Israel, as in other newly industrializing countries, the old generation is identified by the young with the socio-military establishment and with collectivist doctrines. The young generation, on the other hand, is labeled by the old as consumed by American "pop culture" that replaces national ideals and values. Notwithstanding, in Israel the mandatory military service is still the consensus, seen by both old and young as a taken-for-granted national initiation rite. The enlistment of the Israeli citizen serves as the given frame of reference within which smaller, apolitical youth rebellions can be fought.

Youth culture in the large cities, especially Tel-Aviv, has celebrated the idea that the collectivity, the State, and Zionism as a whole need to be bracketed, "forgotten" and shifted aside in order to make room for the individual. Ohad Pishof, a self-declared representative of Israel's first "lost generation" and a leader of a musical group, wrote in 1988:

> In almost every respect, life is not what it used to be. All the grand visions, in our case the grand Zionist vision, prepare us for a vague fulfillment that will never occur, declaring this part of our life, the here and now of life, as a temporary situation, an emergency full of threats whose end nobody can foresee. The paranoid, if true premise, is that our small and brave country is constantly under threat, and this is used as a sneaky pretext for solidarity

and for not doing all that great stuff that we should have already done but did not do, even with five wars behind us.

Pishof was 17 years old when these words were published in a main-stream, leftist-oriented magazine, whose editor, a well-known and well-established journalist (later Israel's consul general to Philadelphia) proclaimed him as the voice of a generation. The "great stuff" Pishof is referring to signifies an American brand of consumerist, hedonist individualism: music, fashion, travel, leisure, MTV, cyberspace, cinema, and outings.

Young Israeli writers and artists were also partaking in this quest for apolitical individualism. Tel-Avivian artists were grouped together under the ticket of "less is more," emphasizing idiosyncrasy and minimalist style over figurative symbolism (the sign of the "old masters"). A "return to infantilism" was similarly advocated in the prose of young writers as an escape from the all-embracing grasp of the political. Gadi Taub, who in 1997 published a book on contemporary Israeli youth culture, terms these trends "the dispirited rebellion." The young generation, according to this thesis, is a rebel with a cause but without determination. Bound by the collectivist discourse of siege and commitment, the young gen-eration expresses its "dispirited rebellion" by partaking in the global importation of popular subcultures, avoiding the political while denouncing the predisposition of the "old generation" with local (iden-tified as parochial, peripheral, outdated) ideals derived from the mod-ernist project of nation-building.

This chapter reads the "dispirited rebellion" of Israeli youth in a popular Israeli film entitled *Late Summer Blues.*[1] The film takes place almost entirely in northern Tel-Aviv of the early 1970s. The heroes of the film are young boys and girls facing army enlistment; the main arena is a high school in the city of Tel-Aviv; the plot pivots on the preparation of the graduation party; and in the background is the war of attrition. One can see at first glance that these dramatic materials present a mixture of local and universal elements. On the one hand, we have a typically Israeli frame of reference: "pre-enlistment." On the other hand, the film's heroes represent an age-group whose youth cul-ture is based on American cultural models. The graduation ceremony, whose contents are distinctly local, is also an example of the universal phenomenon anthropologists call "rites of passage."

Late Summer Blues will not be examined here within the cinematic discipline and genre, but from an external vantage point from which it may be seen as a cultural document. The premise for this approach is that cinema—like literature, poetry, painting and other types of art—reflects to a certain extent the socio-cultural context in which it is created. The representation is not obvious; indeed, it is often vague and indirect. Various methods of analysis are able to trace the outlines of the social and cultural processes reflected in a work, although no method claims to have reached the most correct understanding of the "work's spirit," or, alternatively, the most faithful interpretation of the "author's intentions."[2]

My examination of *Blues* as a cultural document focuses on those processes that play a central role in the film's plot: processes of identity, loss and gain; preserving individuality versus the acceptance of the collective dictate; the struggle between the cosmopolitan alternative hidden in Tel Aviv and the local patriotism it represents. The fact that *Blues* is a very "Tel-Avivian" film and at the same time a very "Israeli" film is therefore an important point. I call *Blues* a "Tel-Avivian film" for reasons which need to be clarified. Many films have been shot in Tel-Aviv locations, but they cannot be termed "Tel-Avivian films." I mean by this term a film where Tel-Aviv is not only its geographical arena, but also its symbolic territory; a film which realizes in Tel-Aviv those things which the city is conceived as symbolizing, renewing, repressing or distorting. In this respect, *Blues* is a Tel-Avivian film just as Uri Zohar's film *Einayim Gdolot* (Big Eyes) is a Tel-Avivian film and Ya'akov Shabtai's novel *Zikhron Dvarim* (Memorandum) is a Tel-Avivian novel. These are works which perceive the city of Tel-Aviv through a symbolic, even mythical, prism of mythic struggles: hedonism versus responsibility; emotional life versus big ideas; the movement's verdict versus the individual's wishes; the glory and promise of the past versus the disintegration and failures of the present; avant-garde versus conformity; creation and renewal versus treading water and loss of selfhood; and so on.

Of course, none of these binary oppositions is limited to the city of Tel-Aviv, since all reflect deep structures in the whole of Israel as well as human society in general. However, it is Tel-Aviv that raises them to the surface, liberates them from their hiding place, provides them with the conditions for their expression, one beside the other, and thus causes their inevitable collision. The city of Tel-Aviv and the country of Israel are not just physical territories; they are symbolic entities, distinguished by their cultural qualities and complementary to each other, with each one separately forming the identity of the individual living in them. While a country is a "big place"—a life world of values, ideas, ambitions and images—a city is a "small place,"[3] a physical, earthly, everyday dwelling place. This does not negate the possibility of the connection between the two, and they may certainly nourish each other, but separation and distancing between them are also possible.

The Plot

The film's main thematic units are four life stories. The first story is that of Yossi Zwillich, who is about to enlist. After the school is informed of the death of one of its graduates, the class takes an exam on Zionism, during which the principal announces the postponement of the graduation ceremony, due to the tragedy. Zwillich protests, claiming he would miss the ceremony due to his recruitment. On the eve of his enlistment, the group holds a farewell party for Zwillich, during which he asks one of the girls to become his girlfriend. She conditions it on his giving her "parachutist's wings," which he promises to bring her. On the following day, his parting from the group and from his parents, at the entry to the recruitment center, is documented by one of the group—Margo. The group goes out to celebrate on the beach and is caught smoking grass, but the members are released from custody, so that their arrest will not place a stain on them in view of their approaching enlistment.

The second story is that of Ahraleh, the rebel among the group, who writes graffiti against the war and against the establishment. During the rehearsal for the graduation ceremony, Ahraleh and his friends sneak into the principal's office, smoke grass there, put a joint to the lips of a photograph of Golda Meir and search for the location of Honduras on the globe. The principal receives a telephone message concerning Zwillich's death in a training accident. Nevertheless, she continues the rehearsal and gives a speech including educational questions, such as: "Are we making correct, fair use of them [the pupils]? Are we preparing them for real life?" Ahraleh protests vigorously that she does not mention Zwillich's death, and walks out to the sound of the principal's response, that "there are some things you don't yet understand." Zwillich's burial is also documented by Margo's camera, and after it the group decides to stage a protest show for the end of the year, a show which will include singing satirical pieces such as "It is good to die for our country" and "We don't want wars, violence, cemeteries." Ahraleh continues to spray protest slogans, is almost caught by the police, and in making his escape reaches the house of Naomi, whom he desires. He finds her in the company of Mossi, reading Zwillich's diary. Kobi and Shoshi, two members of the group, get married. On the beach on their wedding night which they spend with their friends, an argument erupts between Kobi and Ahraleh, during which the latter is accused of cowardice under the guise of idealism. Ahraleh totters on the pier, shouting: "I am a coward!"

The third story is that of Mossi, a talented musician, who is considering joining a military entertainment troop because he falls for a girl who is trying to get into that troop. The troop's commanders visit the graduation ceremony, see Mossi perform and decide to accept him. However, after Ahraleh and his girlfriend Naomi accuse Mossi of betraying the group by exploiting the ceremony for his own needs, Mossi changes his mind and joins the parachutists. His enlistment is also recorded by Margo.

The fourth story is that of Margo, the photographer and director of the documentary films, and the narrator of the film itself. Margo is exempt from military service due to his diabetes. He is willing to do anything in order to be fit for enlistment, but since there is no chance of that, he decides to go to Paris to study cinema. He cannot bear the thought of his friends returning from the army and telling their stories, and the feeling that, following their enlistment, "Tel-Aviv suddenly looks like a deserted city." In Paris he hears about the death of Mossi Bluesmy beloved") in the 1973 Yom-Kippur War. Being requested by Mossi's parents to find for them the documentaries about their son, he returns to Israel. The film ends with the opening pictures: the group is filmed on the beach, with a well-known commemorative poem playing in the background.

Late Summer Blues as a Mythical Structure

When I claim that in *Blues* there are mythical elements, I mean that there is a framework story (narrative) based on relationships of opposites; moreover, these opposites are brought, by means of the dramatic development, into a struggle during which they may reverse and change. This struggle is "mythical" in that it is connected to the hub of the cultural forces which dictate the lives of the individual and of society.

A systematic analysis of the elements of myth hidden in *Blues*, as in its cinematic equivalents—*Chavura Shekazot* (Such a Group), *Metzitzim* (Voyeurs), *Eskimo Limon* (Lemon Lollipop), *Echad Mishlenau*

(One of Us), and others—may reveal a common cultural code, which has developed out of the same social context. To perform the formal analysis of this code—the exposure of the "mythemes," the basic units (pairs of contrasts) of the mythical structure, as Claude Levi-Strauss termed them—we require just two mechanisms. The first mechanism is the one that separates the mythemes and divides them into a series of pairs of contrasts, each pair a thing and its opposite. This mechanism determines borders, defines categories, and creates a pre determined order. The second mechanism, on the other hand, is capable of switching round the two mythemes comprising the pair of opposites. This is a transformative mechanism, turning sacred into secular, individual into subject, youth into man. This mechanism, then, realizes the dynamism of social life and the fluidity and instability of concepts and borders.

The basic scheme for the organization of the script's components can be presented by a system of contrasting dilemmas, each of which leads to the next:

1. The personal versus the social
2. The individual versus the collective
3. The family collective versus the national collective
4. Belonging to a sexual category, women versus men
5. Identification with the present, young people versus the adult past generation
6. Belonging to a national collective versus humanity in general
7. Belonging to a special place versus the cosmos
8. Deciding between historical time and mythical time
9. Choosing between death perceived symbolically as eternal life and death perceived as impotence
10. Existential decision versus the renunciation of meaning

This mythical odyssey colors the script in universal shades and gives it the feel of a story whose development is isolated from the overt plot. The cultural arena of the film is double: on the one hand the city of Tel-Aviv in the summer of 1970, with its beach and its northern neighborhoods, and on the other hand the military-national Israel of the same period. These are two places with different laws. The first is earthly, real, personal, familiar and controllable. The second is abstract, general, collective and fatalist. The first is limited to the everyday and by chronological time; the second is imbued in myth and the cyclical time of "eternal return." In order to read the story of *Blues* we now need to examine how the cinematic drama unfolds along the two axes described: the axis in which cultural limits are defined and emphasized, and the axis in which the binary oppositions on both sides of the divide win, lose or change.

The four life stories comprising the film's composition are apparently personal stories, and even their titles testify to this: "Yossi," "Ahraleh," "Mossi" and "Margo"; however, the content of the stories deals with the systematic location of the lives of these youths within a social framework without which they have no existence as a story. Each one of the youths is, presumably, a person with a background, wishes and connections that distinguish him from the group, but these disappear and are absorbed by his assimilation into the group. The group is, therefore, the justification for the existence of the individual, who confronts (and in fact is forced to confront by the script) a constant choice between his ambitions for self-expression and his assimilation in the group. This conflict is presented to us beginning with Yossi Zwillich, who wants to sleep with a girl and to get a driving license; through the rebellious Ahraleh, who wishes to protest against the existing order and change it; to the creative Mossi, whose artistic identity is subdued to the group's directive; and to Margo, who feels rejected from the Israeli collectivity because he cannot serve in the IDF due to his diabetes.

This first dilemma, in which there are only two choices—the personal versus the social—is the one that dictates the dynamics of the whole story. The group does allow doubts, soul-searching and looking for the right way, but only for a limited period. The intended and indisputable deadline for this period of doubt is the approaching enlistment in the army, from whose ranks one can only be released by death—or, in Margo's case, diabetes. All our heroes—even the black sheep among them, Ahraleh—enlist, and adopt the ethos against which they had wished to rebel. This enlistment is a dramatic and symbolic act of separation from the group, as preparation for the even more extreme cancellation and negation of the private self. The group, in this respect, is just a preparation for the larger group, the army, and above it the state: the State of Israel as a hierarchy of friends and groups.

The Group

The transition from the individual's living space to his annexation by the collective is conducted through the mediating link of the group.

This is a social form which, although not local, has gained a special hold in Israeli culture. Groups of various types, from the labor corps and other communes, through the kibbutz, the youth movement and the cooperative, constitute a melting pot for the fusion of the private into the collective. Group films have become a popular genre in Israel, which undoubtedly reflects Israeli society's frequent (but not necessarily reflexive) concern with the collective ethos. In the film *Such a Group* (directed by Zeev Havatzelet, according to Puchu's book, 1962) an attempt was made to describe a group whose members are flesh and blood. The result, however, is closer to the national collective myth. Burstein describes how, in one of the film's comic scenes,

> The kibbutz's newcomer (Gideon Singer) is annoyed when the Palmach members hide ammunition crates under the plants of his beloved garden and ruin the seedlings he has planted. The film "speaks" about love for the land, but "shows" the opposite: here Singer is playing the role of a contemptible outsider. He is not "in." His love of nature is dwarfed in comparison with the heroic task of liberating the motherland. The newcomer's disaster—the destruction of the garden he has been cultivating with diligence and effort—is not tragic, but comic. It is intended to emphasize the tragedy reserved for those who are "in": those who die for the motherland and the officers who send them to die. At the same time it allows the representation of these heroes as supposedly "naughty," which the film's creators interpret as a human quality which makes the characters flesh and blood. But this three-dimensionality is applied to the whole group and not to its individual members. The naughtiness of the characters is collective. The three loafers (always three—never one), who escape from field training, practice individual infiltration to Tel-Aviv (their natural place) in order to eat ice-cream there. They decide on this together, and later, when they are prevented from participating in a military action, they regret it together. The sin, like the repentance for the sin, does not stem from the individual's will, but from the group's decision. (1990:85)

The fact that the three loafers escape to Tel-Aviv of all places Bluestheir natural place"), is evidently significant. The Tel-Aviv of *Such a Group* is a sanctuary town, a hiding place from the collective's authority, an open place whose entertainment and leisure sites provide, with their anonymity and cosmopolitanism, an alternative for the steaming melting pot of Israeli society. This, of course, is also the alternative offered (or at least represented) by the Tel-Aviv of *Blues*. But the whole of *Blues* takes place in Tel-Aviv, and in this respect "there is nowhere to escape to." On the other hand, in the group in *Blues* there is an attempt to give the various heroes distinguishing characteristics and to round out their characters, in a way that represents some progress since the days of "Such a Group." But the group's authority is not doubted even here. Burstein, whose book is dedicated to the cinematic history of the Israeli portrait, describes how the surrender to the collective ethos gives rise to a collective photographic mode: "It is no wonder," he writes (1990:86), "that close-up faces in the film *Such a Group* are rare and coincidental. Its heroes have to be seen together, and therefore there is usually no choice but for them to be filmed from a distance." This is true also of *Blues*, and especially of the opening and closing scenes, where the group is filmed on the beach, from a distance.

"Individualism" versus "Collectivism"

The "group films" made in Israel are in themselves a genre which deserves its own study (e.g., Gertz 1987; Klein and Klein 1981; Neeman and Zimmerman 1987). These films deal with the question of identification with the collective versus the preservation of the individual's uniqueness. "The group" is therefore a social practice which reproduces the collective ethos, and with great success. In *Such a Group*, all the youths enlisted for training are called "Yosef," and their personal possessions are exposed for all to see as part of the process of their debasement in the face of the collective. Their personal diaries are also turned over to the group, and thus the possibility of personal and private documentation is eliminated. There is no question here of justifying the war or the commitment to the group; this is a reality which is taken for granted, in the face of which all other commitments, and especially the commitment to the family, are negated.

Loyalty to the collective, as represented in the group films, expresses intergenerational continuity, between parents and children and between older and younger siblings. This continuity is expressed in the military service, preferably combat service, and it binds the erupting rebellion with bonds of family loyalty, which feeds on national tribalism. The reasons for enlisting are no longer important and are never discussed. Even if militaristic ideology has ceased to be accepted and even if leadership is perceived as mistaken and lost, the patterns of identification with the collective action still stand. The women, although they wish to raise families and stick to everyday life ("You can't get married in this country without the news in the middle," remarks a woman in the film *Blues*), are also part of the group, and they encourage the men in it to show loyalty for the higher collective expressed by the army. Enlistment in an "elite unit" is considered a criterion for the "masculinity" of a woman's potential partner, and the withdrawal toward personal-artistic fulfillment is done stealthily and deceitfully and is perceived as betrayal. If there is a rebellion, it is largely a dispirited one, taking the form of a farewell to politics. This was the case even in the largest collective protest against the establishment, in the context of the Lebanon War. This protest

> broke the rule of "Be quiet, we are shooting!"—a rule which symbolizes the brushing aside of internal arguments so long as the battle continues. However, the protest did not digress from the pattern of critical obedience—a pattern which allows criticism, but in the end does not translate it into alternative actions or practices. (Helman 1993:273)

This conclusion is also supported from the specific view point of the film *Blues*, which consists entirely of a description of the suppression of individualism by the dominant collective's system of reference: the group, the army, the state, the school, the family. *Blues* represents the adult generation—parents and educators—as an authority which cannot be questioned. This generation is composed of Zwillich's parents, who, despite their mourning, participate in the graduation ceremony; of parents who accompany their children to the recruitment center on their way to the reception and sorting base; of policemen who are willing not to enforce the law on those facing enlistment; and of a principal and secretary who serve as cultural commissars. All these could have been presented as a category opposed to the younger generation, but *Blues*, true in its own way to the collectivist ethos, reproduces and eternalizes their cultural dominance and presents them as guardians of the normative order and the cultural capital of Israeli society.

The combination of a value system that is considered legitimate and is supported by intergenerational links stemming from a feeling of common destiny turns the group into an inescapable cultural trap. Universalistic statements, such as "there are no just wars," perhaps reflect Western youth culture, but have no real echo in the local culture described in the film. The yearning for the extra-Israeli-national world does not represent a constructive alternative, but merely escapism, like that of Margo who goes to Paris to escape the Friday nights when the group will gather for military conversations in which he will have no part.

A Rite of Passage

The graduation party is a rite of passage that leads from school years to military service. For all its prescribed play, it is not surprising to find acts of desecration at the core of the rite of passage. The central stage of such traditional rites, called the liminal stage, involves the desecration of the most holy object of worship in the society—a totem, an image, a certain animal or place.[4] This object is slaughtered, sacrificed, smashed or desecrated. Only after such a desecration has taken place properly can the initiate return to his society, with a new status and identity. The accepted anthropological explanation of this contradiction of holiness and its desecration stems from the assumption that the main power of the rite of passage results from its being a total subjugation of the person's existence to the authority of society and the collective. This subjugation becomes effective through the demonstration of society's power. The peak of this show of power occurs when society proves its ability to smash its own idols. It is not the initiate who desecrates the sanctity, but society, which uses initiates as pawns fulfilling its will.

The graduation play of the heroes of *Blues* is a rite of passage which becomes a parody due to the lack of connection between the myth and the reality in the lives of those youths. The national myth, the hero culture, Zionism, and militarism—all these do not constitute for them the contents of an ordered and clear worldview. They are more like norms and dictates of "see and do." Zwillich dies in the name of the myth, even though his death was not a hero's death, but during a training accident; and Ahraleh enlists despite his doubts concerning the validity of the myths in whose name he might die. Mossi, unlike them, makes a decision based on commitment to the myth as embodied in his brother and family. Margo, forced to watch all of them, is prepared to exchange his diabetes for a recruitment paper.

Living between an exhausted myth and a reality based on other principles does not allow the group to accept Zwillich's death as an integral part of the taken-for-granted mosaic of "Israeli culture." Their feeling is that he died in vain, that he had a death not only biological, but also and mainly social. They cannot hold a memorializing ritual for Zwillich, and on the other hand, they cannot rebel against the chains of the collective which bind them. This lack of ability is the key to understanding the group's existential dilemma. Their dilemma is, in fact, a loyal representation of contemporary Israeli youth culture. The wandering between belonging to the cosmic entities of nation and land on the one hand, and life in the realistic city on the other hand, causes the "large place"—the country—to stand in contrast to the "small place"—the city. The declaration of one of the participants in the school's graduation play, "I have no place to die," is the desperate statement of someone whose maturation places his personal life cycle on the threshold of his society's death cycle.

The "city" and the "country," Tel-Aviv and Israel, are two forms of place and of time, where none of the heroes of *Blues* can find a resting place for himself. Without a place to die, there is also no place to live, and the youths of the group are inevitably absorbed into the collectivity. Their bounded reflexivity, in which irony and nostalgia are mixed in equal doses, testifies above all to the inability of the observer to change his preprogrammed behavior according to the Israeli-tribal code.

The Tel-Aviv Syndrome

One of the phenomena attributed to the spiritual influence of Jerusalem on some of its visitors is known as the "Jerusalem syndrome." This is an agitated mental state, in which the atmosphere of Jerusalem drives the tourist insane and causes him or her to do things and to see hallucinations which they would not have done or hallucinated elsewhere. There is no parallel phenomenon connected with Tel-Aviv.

Jerusalem is a combination of a "small place" and a "large place"; it has myth and eschatology combined with a reality of residence and everyday life. In other words, the heavenly Jerusalem and the earthly Jerusalem are mixed up, and create, for the visitor, a distorted temporal world, in which the boundaries between mythological time and earthly existential time collapse. The lack of coordinates stems from Jerusalem's unique cultural place in the awareness of the historical religions in particular, and in the Western world in general. Tel-Aviv is a place of one time—earthly, local, existential and immediate—a time of mortals, managing their lives along a social life cycle. The other time, the mythical, immortal time, invades this temporal existence in special circumstances, such as an enlistment ceremony. The need to decide between the times arises when the question of the meaning of life and death is raised in the framework of the collective self, and not as part of the private self. The behavioral handling of this question is performed in the group by a reflective game of contrasts, which avoids, by its being a game, a commitment to one time or the other.

Afterword: *Blues* as Simulation

Late Summer Blues simulates an exhausted myth that is both deconstructed and reconstructed by youth culture. The very essence of the "group" is a symbol of collectivism. Moreover, for all its individualism and rebelliousness, the group conforms, at the end of the day, to the plans of the collectivity. This could be taken as the symbolic usurpation of youth by adult Israeli society. The ability—limited from the outset—of the heroes of *Blues* to perform soul-searching before they are incorporated into the collectivity results from their being in a liminal position. They are already out of school, and not yet in the army; no longer boys and not yet men. The maturation of the group occurs at the meeting place of two opposing cultural frameworks. The streets of Tel-Aviv, the school corridors and the beach are earthly environments that one wishes to stick to, so that "it will never end" (as the well-known commemorative poem goes).

Blues is hence a graduation film told from an autobiographical point of view. As such, it is based on reflections and simulations. The youths represent their lives to themselves, to their parents and to their teachers; Yossi Zwillich writes a diary; Ahraleh conducts a graffiti diary on the walls of Tel-Aviv "in order to annoy all those who don't care." But the characters are mainly reflected through the lens of Margo's camera. Margo, the outcast, who is at first considered a nuisance due to his wish to document, becomes the commemorator of the group and its members. The commemorative power of his camera gives Margo a perspective whose exterior is nostalgic but whose essence presents an illusion of "the thing itself." "Were we like that, so stupid, so beautiful, so pure?" asks Margo in his exile, and the process of his alienation from the group is at its strongest at a time when it is he who holds the key to commemoration.

The two faces of Tel-Aviv—the beach and the graffiti-covered streets, collectivist nostalgia and the collective fracture—are welded in *Blues*. The film subscribes neither to a bleak individualistic awareness nor to political and social criticism. In this respect, it ends up with a Hollywood-style, simplistic plot. Here arguably lies the secret of its appeal and popular acceptance; this film was chosen to represent Israel in the Oscar awards competition for the best foreign movie.

The self-reflection methods adopted by the people of *Blues*, just like their brief flights of individualism, are limited in advance by the collective frame of reference. Trapped between Israeli society's "rules of ceremony" on the one hand and its "hero culture" on the other hand, the youths of the group find release for their criticism in a different model of representation: parody. This parody serves both as a distorted mirror of the ceremonial and as a means of rebutting the myths of the "hero culture." As part of the protest play which was not staged, the group's youths present a parody of Yossi Zwillich's taken-for-granted enlistment BluesGet up and join the Hebrew corps"), and even a parody on the character of Yosef Trumpeldor BluesIt is good to die for our country") who represents the collective hero.

The satire on Zwillich's death, desecrating the "sanctum" of Israeli national existence—the myth of the fallen soldier—is presented only as a "rehearsal." It does not move beyond a stage of "simulation," and is not staged in front of the adults. It remains as an exercise, as a possibility of a rebellion which is not realized. In fact, quite the opposite happens. The provocative act of presenting questions concerning the fatalism in Israeli national existence ends with a sort of acceptance of answers which have never been given and whose source is not in accepted reason or logic. This acceptance leads to participation in the inevitable Israeli social practice of memorializing the fallen. The parents, the friends, the school and the whole of society require the continued presence of the dead among them, so that the social life of the deceased will not end with their physical demise.[5]

Reality Check: Rabin's Assassination and Youth Culture

Gadi Taub (1997) opens his account of the apolitical youth culture in contemporary Israel with a very political incident: Rabin's assassination. In Taub's view, Rabin's assassination signified for Israeli youth not only a shock, but also an awakening. It was a moment of crystallization for a generation that consciously and dispiritedly distanced itself from political culture. Taub cites Yosef El-Dror, a young satirical writer, as a typical conveyor of this "moment":

> Suddenly, all of us—disillusioned people, lacking a clear political view, subjects of a disintegrating society—were faced with a massive exposure to a new meaning: "a man who served an idea." It was a strange, old-new thing in the new and vulgar Israeli capitalism. A man who served an idea was murdered, removed, and for a moment you could see the actual idea, the big story behind him.[6]

In other words, it was through his assassination that Rabin became the subject of social consensus and solidarity that could embrace young and old, dispirited and patriotic alike. Rabin's assassination was an emotional snowball that temporarily revived Israeli collectivism. How it did so is the subject of the following chapter.

NOTES

1. The film *Late Summer Blues* was produced in 1987 by Ilan De-Vries, Ranan Shor, and Doron Nesher, and directed by Ranan Shor.
2. The assumptions described here, somewhat simplistically, are those of the post-structuralist approach. Various "methods" are included in this approach, such as the Archaeology of Knowledge (Foucault 1972), Grammatology and Deconstruction (Derrida 1976), the Semiology of Literature (Barthes 1967, 1975), Symbolic Exchanges (Baudrillard 1983), and also mytho-poetic, psychoanalytic approaches and so on. The Death of the Author has already become a sort of axiom of structuralist research (see Foucault 1979), focusing on the reader's position and on the analysis of the text-as-it-is-read in different social situations and historical periods. This "reconstruction" of the text's meaning requires a poetics of acceptance (see Fish 1980; Holub 1984; Iser 1978). The general rationale guiding this research is that there are literary phenomena which cannot be explained fully out of the text itself, "from the inside," but should be interpreted as symptoms whose roots are on a different level, the social and cultural level.
3. The big place and the small place are a pair of terms proposed by Aran and Gurevich (1991), which the present manuscript uses as part of a specific cultural paradigm—of big place/small place = country/city = Israel/Tel-Aviv = collective/individual.
4. These characteristics are borrowed from the important theoretical work of Van Gennep (1969) on rites of passage, a work which Turner (1969) later used and expanded.
5. The eternal life provided to the deceased by means of memorializing ceremonies are in fact the basis of what I call the "hero culture." This term was developed by Becker (1973) and expanded by Lifton (1986). In the specific Israeli context of "hero culture," see the important work of Miron (1992).
6. Yosef El-Dror, Ma'ariv daily newspaper, "Tarbut Ma'ariv" supplementary, 10.11.95.

5. LIVING AFTER THE ASSASSINATION

The Political Discourse

❦

A couple of months after Rabin's assassination on 4 November 1995 by a fellow Israeli and Jew, the following graffiti appeared on a highway next to Bar-Ilan University: "Yisrael machaka et Rabin" (Israel erased Rabin). In Hebrew, the wording of that script evoked a poetic touch since it was a paraphrasing of the popular Six-Day War song, "Nasser machake le-Rabin" (Nasser is waiting for Rabin), which later on, in 1992, was yet again paraphrased to become the Labor Party's leading election campaign slogan: "Yisrael mechaka le-Rabin" (Israel is waiting for Rabin). The three slogans capture a cultural narrative of metamorphosis. First, Rabin the hero of the 1967 Yom-Kippur War; second, Rabin in his 1992 political comeback; and third, Rabin as the slaughtered victim of his own peace process.

It is not the purpose of this chapter to consider the "real" political consequences of the murder. Rather, I wish to examine the sweeping national mourning that followed the assassination. I argue that Rabin's posthumous apotheosis was an attempt at reinstating the injured body social of Israel as a whole.[1] The unprecedented collective mourning that followed the assassination was a reaction to the murderer's intent, namely "forget Rabin." However, the ways in which this mourning took shape also spelled a specific editing of "Rabin" into the national pantheon. The Tel-Aviv square, where the assassination took place, became a metaphorical battle zone between myth and history.

The following is an analysis of Rabin's mourning as a media event, a sequence of public performances reported on in the mass media in the wake of the assassination. It is by no means a step-by-step description of the occurrences that followed Rabin's death. Such a sequential tale would be impossible since events were registered simultaneously and through multimedia channels. It is a media-informed, broadly sketched rendition of the cultural narrative constructed during the first few days after the murder. This account frames the reconstruction of Rabin's social body within the dilemma of myth versus history.[2]

Rabin's Two Bodies

Israel has formulated a ceremonial routine for the laying in and burial of its departed leaders. However, these codes of practice assumed a natural death. No provisions were made for a violent, premature termination of office. The annals of late Israeli presidents and prime ministers and, indeed, of all Israeli political figures include death by natural causes alone and, in the majority of cases, after retirement. The procedures that follow such deaths are designed to secure and maintain a sense of symbolic as well as political continuity.[3] The immediate predicament engendered by the assassination was how to preserve cultural permanency in the midst of a breakdown. The very burial of Rabin's body signified the burial of the body politic. The dilemma was how to bury Rabin without burying the "dream."

The solution to that dilemma was in symbolic immortality. A reediting of certain elements in Rabin's biography projected a new version of cultural hero. That symbolic creation enlisted only those constituents in Rabin's life-story which were not commensurate with the assassin's ideological stance. Hence any reminiscence of Jewish nationalism was systematically expurgated from the mythical rebuilding of Rabin's "legacy." The murdered Rabin that emerged out of the shattered Zionist ethos was one possessing civil, humanistic and universal traits rather than a culturally specific character upholding fundamentalist values.

First, there were the events surrounding the temporary disappearance of Rabin's body. Amidst the total confusion that struck the media at the moment of the assassination, the prime minister's own body temporarily disappeared. The grand finale of the peace rally with both

Rabin and Peres joining in the exhilarated chanting of the "Song for Peace" projected the two leaders as part of an indivisible collective body overarching and effacing personal and political differences.[4] It should be noted that the lyrics of the song call to bury the dead who cannot be returned to life and instead to bring a future of peace. This plea to overlook the past and not to dwell on the cult of the fallen soldier was regarded, at the time of the first performance of the song (after the Six-Day War), as a heretic act and in fact, following public protest was banned from the state-controlled media for a while. The repudiation of biological death sung by Rabin only a few moments before his own demise contributed a great deal to the inclusion of that song in the canon of his posthumous myth.

Rabin's body disappeared from the public eye and was rushed to a hospital without any media monitoring. In fact, the private body never reverted to the social one. It was "snatched" to the hospital not to reappear in any physical form. With no transitory passage of dying, Rabin's body skipped the transformation from the corporeal to the social. Rather, it preempted biological terminality by entering symbolic immortality. A second condition emerging upon the murder and enabling the subsequent work of myth making was the public preoccupation with the status of words. It was almost as soon as the news on the assassination reached the media that attention was poignantly directed to the role of words in paving the way to the plausibility of the event. Whether or not it was politically geared or culturally motivated, sweeping sensitivity to the accountability of incitement in legitimizing the murder was hyped by all media. While socialist Zionism was known to separate words from deeds, discounting the former and emphasizing the latter,[5] the opposite linkage occurred following the murder—speech and action were suddenly deemed one.[6]

The controversy precipitated a social atmosphere where any haphazard utterances could be quickly labeled as incitement. Outright accusations were leveled at expressions made by right-wing leaders prior to the murder. The refusal of Rabin's widow to receive condolences from such figures and her unequivocal charge that by word of mouth they instigated the murderer and legitimized his reasoning, left a resounding impact on the media. This was borne out by the assassin who kept making statements citing phrases and slogans taken from the overt ideology of the Right, brandished at their mass demonstrations.

The cultural premium put on the significance of the word rendered any usage of speech or writing mythical. The fusion between narrative and performance, speech and act is one of the basic features of the mythical, where historical time is suspended to be superseded by "totemic time"[7]—total identification with a core cultural trope. The supposed sacredness of such experience leads to an unreserved commitment to mass participation in the public worship of the mythical object. Such participation, being a public performance by nature, requires the copresence of fellow worshippers, a presence which must be anchored in designated sites. The rites of the cult of the dead Rabin took place in three major locations where his newly constructed biography could be engraved. In effect, three sanctified sites of mass pilgrimage[8] were selected to generate and sustain the emerging myth, and merged into one metaphorical burial ground, the "State of Israel."

The three sites of Rabin's commemoration were Rabin's family home (reflecting the Judaic lineage kinship system); the Tel-Aviv square where the murder was committed (a place representing urban, secular Israel); and the grave at Mount Herzl[9] (superseding the ancestral, biblical Jerusalem with the pantheon of nation builders in earthly Jerusalem). These three sites of public performance of burial rites drew hundred of thousands worshippers in a threefold pilgrimage journey. Notwithstanding certain variations in the distribution of the crowds attending the three respective sites, the overall circulation of visits encompassed a large portion of the population regardless of age, ethnic origin, gender, or faith. It should be noted, however, that the family home and the square were frequented mainly by youngsters.

"Our Father Has Gone"

The cultural work of rewriting Rabin's biography commenced almost upon the time of the murder. It took the media, in particular the TV authorities, only a couple of hours after the initial shock to produce and broadcast extensive archive footage of Rabin's political career, of which two epochs were distinctly highlighted: the War of Independence and the current era of peacemaking. The interrelatedness was particularly evident when the young Rabin was presented as the complementary side of his old counterpart, hence closing a life cycle of war and peace. That was indeed the foundation for the emergence of Rabin's image as a sacrificial son-cum-patriarch[10] whose nation-building enterprise is encapsulated within his entire life course. The mixing of the youthful commander and the elderly statesman was a theme running through the media presentation of Rabin's biography.

It is important to mention at this point that Rabin's functioning in the Six-Day War (1967) as chief of staff was underplayed. Prior to Rabin's death several attempts were made to undermine his contribution to the two wars. Recounts of his alleged nervous breakdown during the 1967 War were regarded as legitimate, carried some weight in public opinion and were exploited by the right wing in their 1992 election campaign. The other attempt, relating to the War of Independence, although heavily documented and very timely,[11] did not seem to capture the gaze of the media and caused very few ripples. The explanation to this difference might rest with the cultural representation projected by either image. The "War of Independence Rabin" was a one and all time icon of the mythical *Sabra*, "The Silver Tray"[12] upon which the Jewish State was delivered to the nation.

During the Six-Day War, however, Rabin was already a replaceable icon whose attributes were embedded in the military machinery that won the war. Thus the two pioneering figures—that of the *Sabra* and that of the peacemaker—were aligned to transmit a character of unique features and indispensable presence in the life of the nation. Rabin's death was conveyed as the loss of that perennial figure. His role in the Israeli imagined community was that of an eternally youthful forefather whose demise could be likened to paternal abandonment.

The key metaphor embracing the whole gamut of mourning practices revolved around that axis of father-children relationship. Expressions such as "We have lost our father," "We are now orphans," "Why have you gone from us father?" were rife. To mourn the dead father, the media established two interlocking protagonists: the mourning youth and the mourning family. The radio and TV swiftly moved from one locus to another to create a burial ground where the young were omnipresent. Notwithstanding the evident presence of other generations, interviewers and cameras sought and caught the behavior of youngsters, from toddlers through school children, adolescents and persons in their early twenties. Older mourners were given merely scant screen space, unless shown in the company of the young.

To understand the role of the youthful, it is necessary to analyze the symbolic language of mourning that was heard and seen in the media. The vocabulary of that language consisted of a few major cues which together constituted a grammar of public mourning hitherto unknown in Israel. Even though no new symbol was invented for the occasion, the new context endowed familiar codes with different meanings.

Rabin's Family

Whereas the widow had already been a well-known public figure, the children and the grandchildren remained, until the murder, relatively anonymous. The discovery of the second and third generations by the media was sparked off by the granddaughter's eulogy at the grave. That rendition was presented as the emotional peak of the funeral, overshadowing all other tributes paid by the illustrious galaxy of world leaders attending the burial. It is interesting to observe that the runner-up for that status of the most moving eulogy was King Hussein's emotive speech in which he employed terms of putative kinship, calling the widow "my sister" and Rabin "my brother." Furthermore, in that rank of familiarization Clinton's phrase of "Shalom Haver" (Goodbye friend) scored highly too, and has become a buzzword engulfing the country in the form of graffiti, car stickers and street posters. Rabin was thus reconstructed in the ideal type of a family man—a brother, a husband, a flesh and blood father, and a loving, caring and warm grandfather. His two grandchildren made a few TV appearances where they refused to discuss the political implication of the murder and concentrated on jovial enactment of family scenes.

Rabin the family man was an image with which mourners could identify personally. This by no means contradicted his cultural production as the archetype of the *Sabra*. Conversely, these are complementary, grounded in the familiar, the popular, and the commonsensical. The dual image of Rabin strengthened the tenuous link between the tarnished and alienating Zionist ethos and the everyday life of Israelis.

Songs

The peace and death rally preceding the murder ended with a sing-along of the "Song for Peace" with Rabin seen to be humming it. In the course of the gathering a few artists went on stage to express sympathy to the cause and to perform. The most notable of those was Aviv Geffen—an enormously popular, albeit controversial, rock star whose outrageous lyrics often provoked public outcry. In the rally he presented a song of farewell to a dead friend, "to cry for you." One of the immediate responses to the assassination was the adoption of both songs as commemorating hymns. Other well-known songs were selectively added to the litany of mourning to compose an almost canonized body of verse. All those songs were elegiac odes, intertextually connected by virtue of their cultural status as established lyrics expressing the contact between peace, death and locality.[13] The effect of that corpus was further dramatized and halved by the revelation that a blood-drenched script of the "Song for Peace" was found in Rabin's pocket.

Flowers

The culture of flowers (cf. Goody 1994) is highly germane to the understanding of the Zionist ethos. Bridled nature stands for the right of Zionism to claim the land and to settle it, while at the same time protecting it from that very conquest (cf. Arieli 1994). Celebrations of flowers are conducted in special festivals where garlands crown children's heads. Protection of wild flowers is regarded as a highly important educational teaching and the laying of wreaths is a ceremonial constituent at state funerals and commemorative events. Flowers also carry a general value of aesthetics and the taming of nature. This combination between the local and the global might account for the proliferation of flower laying in the mourning rituals. Flowers signify an added dimension of being an emblem of the hippie culture of rebellious adolescents. This symbolic quality encompassing global culture, local knowledge and age-related tropes is also embedded in the following practice of candle lighting.

Candles

It would be difficult to overestimate the cultural significance of candle lighting in Jewish tradition (cf. Sered 1991). From Sabbath candles, through the lighting of candles in saints' tombs, the symbol of the Menorah[14] to commemoration candles, candles are one of the most prominent artifacts of Jewish religion as well as of domestic tradition. It would be analytically futile to sift through the influence borne by the mourners while lighting their candles. To confound that symbolic picture, the part that candles play in pop-rock concerts must also be considered as yet another source of cultural inspiration. The fact is that the three sites of pilgrimage were shown to be places of massive candle lighting. Evidently, the visibility and the distinctiveness of this practice made for its salience in the media, but among equally dazzling images of flowers, youth and graffiti, the candles certainly stole the limelight. The interpretation of the motif of light within the context of youth culture gains further grounds while being juxtaposed to another youth-related practice—the graffiti.

Graffiti

The fusion of fire and words has been a longstanding ceremonial code among Israeli youth movements. Fire inscriptions displayed burning slogans of devotion and commitment to a variety of Zionist credos. Rabin's mourners differentiated between the two and reserved the scripts to the graffiti. Political protest graffiti occasionally and sporadically appear on Israeli city walls but the practice has never gained the fierce and widespread momentum it claims in the urbanite modern world. In that respect the use of graffiti to express views and feelings in the wake of the murder could be regarded as a cultural novelty.

The center of graffiti scribbling was, by nature of the sites, the square where the assassination took place. That square which was renamed after Rabin (instead of Kings of Israel Square) became the drawing board of ideas, protestations, emotive verses of anguish and exchanges of ideological positions. The imposing building of the Tel-Aviv town hall overlooking the square lent its enormous walls to the artists and displayed their work uncensored. It should be noted that a couple of months after the murder a member of the city council (incidentally of leftist views) demanded—in the name of aesthetics—the cleaning up of the building. That encountered a broad opposition which in turn prevented the operation from taking place. The surge of graffiti writing was confined to the place of the square and to the time of public mourning.

The unique and ad hoc pattern of mourning formed after the assassination calls for an explanation. I argue that whatever the long-term repercussions might be, the emergence of that bereavement culture was an experiment in rewriting the Zionist myth. The above observations reveal a code which was neither haphazard nor planned.

Afterword: Rabin's Bereavement as Simulation

What did Rabin's bereavement represent? The people who participated in the emergent cult of the dead Rabin also embarked on an exploratory venture of reconstructing their own identity. This participation, although intensive and meaningful, was ephemeral and noncommitted; I therefore conceive of it as yet another form of simulation. The most blatant feature of the cult of the dead Rabin was a cultural reversal. A young and disillusioned generation, previously disinterested in politics and "big ideas," was suddenly making a political stand. This represented a return to—or perhaps a simulation of—old and "mythical" days when youth movements mobilized their members to perform voluntary feats for the service of the Nation. For the young and dispirited Israelis, Rabin's death revived collectivist values and themes long discounted and discredited in Israeli society. The retrieval of the *Sabra* symbol in the image of Rabin offered what seemed to be a sane and secular collectivist ethos, far from the extreme nationalism of the religious right.

While many Israelis mourned Rabin, it was the mourning of the youth that attracted particular attention, mainly because of its collective and ritualistic nature (see also Raviv et al. 1998 for a psychological analysis). What did the mourning of Rabin by Israeli youth mean? As the youth did not provide an answer to this riddle, it had to be explained by others. For adults, the marriage between the omnipresence of youth, and the media production of the youthful Rabin—the eternal *Sabra*—became a springboard for the restoration of Israel's formative era. The spontaneous and unexplained bereavement of youth was hence usurped by middle-age society. Israeli society—about 50 years old and suffering from an acute midlife crisis—usurped Rabin's bereavement, particularly by the youth, and turned it into an act of self-rejuvenation.

The ritual, however, was not without paradoxes. The performance at the death sites expressed confusion and turmoil—a state not unfamiliar to adolescents. The sense of loss of direction was also well-asserted in some of the graffiti. Two examples will suffice: "Rabin, the bullets that hit you hit all of us"; and the ultimate reprobation: "Yigal Amir—why have you done this to us?" In the midst of the shambles of the social body, other graffiti called for its reconstitution through an apotheosis of the dead leader. It pronounced that "Now there is a God in heaven." This new version of mythical thinking dislodged Judaism from the core of the Zionist ethos and replaced it with a secular hero. The attempt to deify Rabin could attest to a desire to recapture Zionism as an integral ethos.

However, there is empirical evidence that Rabin's death was actually a catalyst for the identity formation of left-oriented youth. The murder had a clear political meaning, and while the media have construed it as a national calamity bereaved by all Israelis, it is logical to assume that supporters of the Left have experienced more intensive emotions of grief and bereavement for Rabin (see Raviv et al. 1998:274). Various surveys were administered to Israeli youth following the assassination (see Yuchtman-Yaar et al. 1998; Ya'ar 1998). The following figures represent the common findings of these surveys. Seventy percent of the youth who responded to the surveys agreed that Rabin's assassination was a "serious social and national crisis." However, when broken down according to religious belief and political orientation, replies showed considerable variance. Of the religious youth surveyed, 38.6 percent agreed that for them, "Rabin's assassination was a sad event, like any murder, but it didn't shake my confidence in the state of Israel." Of the youth defined as "traditional," 28.4 percent also agreed with this option, and so did only 19 percent of the secular youth. In contrast, 65.7 percent of the secular youth, agreed that "Rabin's assassination was a breaking point that shook my confidence in Israeli society" (50 percent of the religious youth, 60 percent of the traditional youth). Religious youth in Israel, it should be noted, are associated with nationalist, right-wing political attitudes, while secular youth are more associated with leftist attitudes.

Furthermore, the peace-oriented group grew in numbers following Rabin's assassination; many of the new activists were adolescents, who seemed to have been moved from indifference to support of Rabin's policies. The paradox here is that it was the Likud (right-wing) Party, rather than the Labor (Rabin's) Party, which won the elections a few months after the assassination. But then again, most of the youth (especially the "candles youth," 15- to 18-year-olds at the time of the assassination) who mourned Rabin did not have a vote in those elections. In the final analysis, then, the most common reaction of Israeli youth to Rabin's assassination was a feeling of sadness and graveness, because a "prime minister was murdered." For the majority of youth, this feeling was also reflected in a loss of confidence in the State of Israel, that is, a loss of confidence in the national establishment. Further reactions depended on political orientations. The assassination seemed to have strengthened existing political orientations while also moving many adolescents from indifference to a support of Rabin's (leftist) policies. This political differentiation means more political conflict. Against the simulation, by the media, of Rabin's bereavement as a national rite of rejuvenation and consensus, the actual reality was therefore one of political and national conflict.

NOTES

1. The concept of the body social alludes to the symbolic position of the human body in cultural discourse as well as to metaphorical configurations of society in corporeal terms. For some recent recapitulation and discussion of the vast corpus of literature on the concept, see Shilling (1993); Synnott (1995).
2. The account is inspired by Handelman's treatment of public events (1990) and by Katz and Dayan's approach to media events (1994).
3. Kantorowicz's description of the double burial of medieval kings exemplifies a practice designated to sustain uninterrupted continuity despite the death of a monarch (1957).
4. The fierce hostility between the two leaders was poignantly expressed in Rabin's autobiography, A Service Diary.
5. The ideology of "practice rather than preach" has gained immense popularity in Israeli political culture. Its origin is attributed to the pragmatic approach of Ben-Gurion's leadership.
6. The indivisible fusion between speech and action goes back to some of the fundamental idioms of Zionism. Katriel (1986) argues that "talking straight" or Dugri culture was one of the principles of the pre-State epoch.
7. Totemic time is an achronological state of sacredness governed by myth and cyclical rhythms. For an analysis of Israeli "totemic" time, see Paine (1983).
8. Mass pilgrimage is described as a journey toward the accomplishment of a collective myth. See, for example, Myerhoff (1974); Turner and Turner (1978).
9. The Mount Herzl national cemetery in Jerusalem is the burial ground for Israeli nation-builders. With the exception of Ben-Gurion, who was interred at his Negev kibbutz, all other heads of state are buried there.
10. The explicit association to the binding of the ancestor Yitzhak is self-evident.
11. For example, U. Milstein, Rabin's File—How the Myth Was Inflated (1995, in Hebrew).
12. A poetic metaphor by Alterman that has become one of Israel's cultural idioms in the symbolic language of commemorating the fallen.
13. These songs were collated and issued on a CD disk, collectively titled Shalom, Chaver, as part of the postmurder memorabilia.
14. The symbol of the Temple; a seven-branched Menorah appears at the center of the emblem of the Israeli state.

EPILOGUE

⸎

Many of the chapters in this book deal with media representations offered by and to Israeli youth—such as TV programs ("This Is It in the Gulf War"), films (*Late Summer Blues*), educational handbooks (for Holocaust tours), and commemoration rituals that were triggered by Rabin's assassination. My reference to youth "culture throughout these chapters has been so far loosely adumbrated. I am not dealing here with the *culture of youth* in a positivist or phenomenological way, as is commonly practiced in sociology (Furnham and Stacey 1991; Manning and Truzzi 1972). "Youth culture," in contrast, is glimpsed here through its reflections: media programs offered to the youth, staged productions that capture and simulate the relationship between Israeli youth and Israeli society.

I have mentioned the reflections of young Israeli writers, who comment on the "dispirited rebellion" of youth in Israel. This metaphor joins well into my discussion of the simulation, since a dispirited rebellion is itself a simulation of intergenerational conflict, which is conducted in the framework of a wider, taken-for-granted acknowledgement of the hegemony of the adult collectivity, whose political culture can be temporarily dodged but never completely evaded. This book describes Israeli youth as a "postmodern" social enclave, whose reality—much like the reality of global youth—consists of leisure simulations and staged productions. Israeli youth, seen through these simulations, is neither fully committed nor fully disengaged, but rather floats between these two polarities in a virtual state of a "non-committal commitment."

A brief tour among the various "simulated dreams" presented in the book should recapitulate their linkage to youth culture. The first chapter describes the "simulated dream" of community, where leading residents (mostly of Oriental origin), backed up by the governmental "Project Renewal," attempt to replace the reality of their poor urban neighborhood with the image of a cosmopolitan community. The original dream, represented in the "melting pot" doctrine of the 1950s and 1960s, promised a culturally homogenous Israeli society that would be molded from its various ethnic constituencies. The residents of Arod in the 1980s were already aware of the failure of that doctrine; a failure of which Arod was direct evidence. Arod's leaders, working together with Project Renewal staff, were interested in the symbolic redemption of Arod. Their project—whose apex were the anniversary programs—was to simulate, through such programs, the shift of Arod from the stigma of "Second Israel" and into the cosmopolitan realm of "First Israel."

Arod's youth had a dual role in that rite of passage. On the one hand, youngsters were among the major performers in the enactment of community. The anniversary program included, for example, dances and other performances by local youth movements. The simulated "community" was thus represented by youth. In contrast, youth also represented the "dark side" of the poor neighborhood. Some of the youth had criminal records that were part of Arod's stigma. Just before the anniversary, the whole neighborhood was "shocked" in view of a TV documentary that depicted the problems of an Arod youth who could not be conscripted into the military. The images associated with youth are thus two-pronged—both a promise for a better future and a reminder of harsh realities.

The second chapter deals with educational handbooks that offer "simulations of the Holocaust" to high-school students. Here, Israel's youth are initiated into its national culture. In the third chapter, a popular TV program aimed for a young audience presents its historical narrative of Israel's ordeal of survival. In chapter four, the analysis of a youth film presents the dialectics of individualism and collectivism in the life of high-school students facing military service. The last chapter recounts the commemoration of Rabin by Israeli youth. While the Israeli media usurped the bereavement rituals of the youth and portrayed them as a national rite of rejuvenation and consensus, the actual reality was one of political and national conflict.

All chapters portray the interplay between the myth and its simulations, the local legacy of the Zionist dream and the impact of global, popular, apolitical and secular culture. It is an interplay between the local and the cosmopolitan (Arod), the national and the diasporic (the Holocaust), left and right (Rabin), the individual and the collective (*Late Summer Blues*). It is perhaps no coincidence that youth should serve as the carrier of that interplay. By nature of its liminal position in the social structure, youth enjoys a social license to experiment with global culture; at the same time, society expects youth to follow its footsteps. Youth is thus always faced with the burden of generativity and the desire to "make it new." It is the local combination of myths and simulations that determines the extent of youth rebellion. In certain times and places, this rebellion is politically informed; in other times and places, youth rebels by being apolitical.

Thus situated, the social representations offered by and to the youth in Israel serve to throw into relief a larger process of change. Israeli society—52 years old in 2000—has been undergoing a process of change in the last decades that undermines its ideological and institutional foundations. Among these changes there is a growing process of sectorialization, which means the weakening of solidarity and democratic consensus. The most shocking expression of this process was the political assassination of Prime Minister Rabin. However, expressions of sectorialization and growing alienation and violence were apparent even before the assassination.

These winds of change stand in contrast to the not-so-distant reality of solidarity and commitment that characterized early Israeli society. Goals concerning the security of Israel and the preservation of its Jewish, secular and democratic character were promoted in the formative years of the State despite the heterogeneity of Israeli society. In general, the ideological basis of Israeli solidarity hinged on Zionism and its goals, that were defined early in the twentieth century. Having been born into a reality in which the original Zionist goals of state-sovereignty, independence, security and economic transformation have been (at least superficially) achieved, it is perhaps little wonder that Israeli youth have begun to look at Zionism as anachronistic. While the youth are involved in identity searches, their life experiences are still controlled and usurped, to a large extent, by middle-age society.

The representations of youth culture suggest that Israeli society is concerned not only with myth debunking, on the one hand, and identity reformation, on the other. It is also, and perhaps to a larger extent, involved in a process that works in-between the debunking or empowering of myths; a process of simulating Zionist myths, reimagining and interpreting them in new ways and with new voices. The sociology of Israeli society should learn how to undo these various anecdotes of self-expression by disentangling their previously monolingual line of interpretation. This is a task already successfully performed by the subjects of socio-anthropological research. Israelis, already involved in the weaving and unweaving of the Zionist ethos, enter and exit at will its fabricated simulations.

In this respect, the Zionist myths are no longer captivating nor are they mandatory constituents in a collective rite of passage towards national identity. Rather than "life events," the media events discussed in this book represent capsules of suspended ideologies. Within such simulations, nationalism is devoid of commitment, Jewishness is without continuity, and bodies are selfless. Simulated Zionism becomes a site for tourist-like nostalgic excursions rather than a "total destination" for pilgrimage. Hence the global shapes the local and the discourse of quintessential myths is overridden by postmodern simulations.

Simulated dreams, therefore, are vehicles by which previously constituted myths generating imagined communities are transformed into fragments of collective imagination. Those virtual relics of the past are no longer effective in rallying national campaigns of wars, absorption of mass immigration or colonizing new frontiers. Rather they are shredded into pieces of cultural idioms, buzz-words, ironical slogans, and recreational venues. In other words, once generative myths, the grand narratives of the drama of Zionism have been turned into disenchanted rituals of pastime and fun.

REFERENCES

Almog, Oz. 1994. "The 'Sabra'—A Sociological Profile" (*Ha-tsabar—Dyokan Sociologi*). Unpublished Ph.D. dissertation, University of Haifa (in Hebrew).
———. 1992. "Monuments for the Fallen Soldier in Israel—A Semiotic Analysis," *Megamot* 34:179–210 (in Hebrew).
Anderson, Benedict. 1983. *Imagined Communities: Reflections on the Origin and Spread of Nationalism*. London: New Left Books.
Aran, Gideon, and Zeli, Gurevitch. 1991. "On Place: Israeli Anthropology" *(Al Hamakom: Anthropologia Yisraelit) Alpayim*, 9–44 (Hebrew).
Arieli, Daniela. 1994. "Cultural Construction of Nature: The Case of the Society for the Protection of Nature." M.A. dissertation, Tel-Aviv University (in Hebrew).
Aronoff, Myron S. 1984. "*Gush Emunim*: The Institutionalization of a Charismatic, Messianic Religious Political Revitalization Movement in Israel." *Religion and Politics, Political Anthropology*, vol. 3. New Brunswick: Transaction Books.
Avrahami, Arza, and Yechezkel Dar. 1993. "Collectivistic and Individualistic Motives among Kibbutz Youth Volunteering for Community Service." *Journal of Youth and Adolescence* 22 (6 Dec.): 697–714.
Avruch, K.A. 1979. "*Gush Emunim*: Politics, Religion and Ideology in Israel," *Middle East Review* 11:26–31.
Azaryahu, Maoz. 1995. *State Cults*. Beer Sheva: Ben-Gurion University of the Negev Press (in Hebrew).
———. 1992. "War Memorial and the Commemoration of the Israeli War of Independence, 1948–1956." *Studies in Zionism* 13(1):57–77.
Apffel-Marglin, F., and S.A. Marglin. 1990. *Dominating Knowledge: Development, Culture and Resistance*. Oxford: Clarendon Press.
Asad, Talal (ed.). 1973. *Anthropology and the Colonial Encounter*. NY: Humanities Press.
Bar-On, Dan, and O. Sela. 1991. "The Psychosocial Effects of the Holocaust in Third and Second Generation Israel." Ben-Gurion University, Dept. of Behavioural Sciences (in Hebrew).
Barthes, Roland. 1967. *Writing Degree Zero*. London: Jonathan Cape.
———. 1972. *Mythologies*. New York: Hill and Wang.

————. 1975. *S/Z, the Pleasures of the Text.* London: Jonathan Cape.

————. 1979. "From Work to Text." In J. V. Harari (ed.), *Textual Strategies: Perspectives in Post-Structuralist Criticism,* pp. 73–81. Ithaca: Cornell University Press.

Bashara, Azmi. 1993. "On the Question of the Palestinian Minority in Israel." *Theory and Criticism,* 3. Jerusalem: Van Leer Institute (in Hebrew).

Baudrillard, Jean. 1983 [1975]. *Simulations.* New York: Semitext(e).

————. 1988. *The Ecstasy of Communication.* New York: Semiotext.

————. 1991. *La Guerre du Golf n'a pas eu Lieu* [The Gulf War did not take place]. Paris: Galilee.

Bauman, Zygmunt. 1992. *Mortality, Immortality and Other Life Strategies.* Cambridge: Polity Press.

Beck, Ulrich. 1992. *Risk Society: Towards a New Modernity.* Trans. by M. Ritter. London: Sage.

Becker, Ernst. 1973. *The Denial of Death.* New York: The Free Press.

Beit-Halachmi, Benjamin. 1992. *Original Sins: Reflections on the History of Zionism and Israel.* London: Pluto Press.

Ben Ari, Eyal. 1993. "Masks and Soldiering: The Israeli Army and The Palestinian Uprising." *Cultural Anthropology* 44, 372–389.

Ben Ari, Eyal, and Yoram Bilu. 1997. *Grasping Land: Space and Place in Contemporary Israeli Discourse and Experience.* Albany, New York: State University of New York Press.

Ben-David, A., and Y. Lavee. 1992. "Families in the Sealed Room: Interaction Patterns of Israeli Families during SCUD Missile Attacks." *Family Process* 31:35–44.

Ben-Eliezer, Uri. 1995. "A Nation-in-Arms: State, Nation and Militarism in Israel's First Years." *Comparative Studies in Society and History* 37:264–285.

————. 1988. "Militarism, Status and Politics." Ph.D. thesis, Tel-Aviv University (in Hebrew).

————. 1995. *The Emergence of Israeli Militarism, 1936–1956.* Tel-Aviv: Zmora Bitan (in Hebrew).

Ben-Gurion, David. 1957. "Concepts and Values." In *Chazut* [Visions]. Tel-Aviv: Mapay Publications (in Hebrew).

————. 1960. "The Eichmann Case as Seen by Ben-Gurion." *The New York Times Magazine,* 18 Dec.: p. 1 ff.

Bennet, John W., and John Bowen (eds.). 1988. *Production and Autonomy: Anthropological Studies and and Critiques of Development.* Lanham, MD: University Press of America.

Ben-Yehuda, Nachman. 1995. *The Masada Myth: Collective Memory and Mythmaking in Israel.* Madison, WI: University of Wisconsin Press.

Ben-Zadok, Efraim. 1993. "National and Spatial Divisions in Israel." In *Local Communities and the Israeli Polity,* Efraim Ben-Zadok (ed.), pp. 1–39. Albany, NY: SUNY Press.

Bilu, Yoram, and Henry Abramovitch. 1985. "In Search of the *Saddiq:* Visitational Dreams among Morrocan Jews in Israel." *Psychiatry* 48:83–92.

Bilu, Yoram, and Eyal Ben Ari. 1992. "The Making of Modern Saints: Manufactured Charisma and the *Abu-Hatseiras* of Israel." *American Ethnologist* 19:672–688.

Burgin, Victor. 1996. *In Different Spaces: Place and Memory in Visual Culture.* Berkeley: University of California Press.

Burstein, Yigal. 1990. *The Face as a Battlefield: The Cinematic History of the Israeli Face* (*Panim Kisde Krav*). Tel Aviv: Hakibbutz Ha'meuhad (in Hebrew).

103

Caplan, Pat. 1988. "Engendering Knowledge: The Politics of Ethnography." *Anthropology Today* 4(5):8–12; 4(6):14–17.

Carmon, Arik. 1980. *Ha'Shoah* [The Holocaust], 2 vols., Jerusalem: Ma'alot (Ministry of Education) (in Hebrew).

———. 1988. "Teaching the Holocaust in Israel." In *Methodology in the Teaching of the Holocaust,* Z. Garber (ed.), Cap. 4. Berlin: Praeger.

Carmon, Naomi, and M. Hill. 1984. "Project Renewal: An Israeli Experiment in Neighborhood." *Habitat International* 8:117–132.

Carrithers, Michael. 1992. *Why Humans Have Cultures.* Oxford: Oxford University Press.

Chomsky, Noam. 1992. "What War?" In *Triumph of the Image: The Media's War in the Persian Gulf—A Global Prespective,* Mowlana et al. (eds.). Boulder, CO: Westview Press.

Clifford, James. 1983. "On Ethnographic Authority." *Representations* 1(2):118–146.

———. 1986. "On Ethnographic Allegory." In Clifford and Marcus (eds.) 1986, pp. 98–121.

Clifford, James, and George Marcus (eds.). 1986. *Writing Culture: The Poetics and Politics of Ethnography.* Berkeley: University of California Press.

Cohen, Anthony. 1982. *Belonging: Identity and Social Organization in British Rural Cultures.* Manchester: Manchaster University Press.

Cohen, Anthony Paul. 1985. *The Symbolic Construction of Community.* London: Chichester.

Cohen, Paul. 1973. "Theories of Myth," *Man* 4: 337–351.

Connerton, P. 1989. *How Societies Remember.* Cambridge: Cambridge University Press.

Danet, Barbara, Yael Loshitzky, and H. Bechar-Israeli. 1993. "Masking the Mask: An Israeli Response to the Threat of Chemical Warfare." *Visual Anthropology.*

Denzin, Norman K. 1991. *Images of Postmodernism: Social Theory and Contemporary Cinema.* London: Sage.

de Lauretis, Teresa. 1984. *Alice Doesn't: Feminism, Semiotics, Cinema.* Bloomington: Indiana University Press.

Derrida, Jaque. 1976. *Of Grammatology.* Baltimore: Johns Hopkins University Press.

Deshen, Shlomo. 1975. "On Religious Change: The Situational Analysis of Symbolic Action." *Comparative Studies in Society and History* 12:260–274.

———. 1993. "Doves, Hawks and Anthropology: The Israeli Debate on Middle Eastern Settlement Proposals." In *Beyond Boundaries,* G. Palsson (ed.), pp. 58–74. Boulder, CO: Sage.

Doane, M.A. 1987. *The Desire to Desire: The Woman's Film of the 1940s.* Bloomington: Indiana University Press.

Doner, Batya. 1991. *Real Time: The Gulf War—Graphic Texts.* Exhibition's catalogue, Tel Aviv Museum of Art, n. 4.91.

Douglas, Mary. 1966. *Purity and Danger.* New York: Penguin Books.

———. 1973. *Natural Symbols.* New York: Pantheon Books.

———. 1997. *Natural Symbols.* New edition. London: Routledge.

Eisenstadt, Shmuel N. 1985. *The Transformations of Israeli Society: An Essay in Interpretation.* London: Weidenfeld and Nicholson.

Elboym-Dror, Rachel. 1996. "He is Coming, from within Us He is Coming: The New Hebrew—On the Youth Culture of Early Immigration to Israel" *Alpayim* 12:104–136 (in Hebrew).

Eliade, Mircea. 1965. *The Myth of Eternal Return.* Bulingen Series, N.Y.

————. 1969. *Images and Symbols: Studies in Religious Symbolism.* New York, Sheed and Ward.

Elon, Amos. 1979. *The Israelis: Founders and Sons.* New York: Holt, Rinehart and Winston.

El-Or, Tamar. 1990. *Educated and Ignorant: On Ultra-Orthodox Women and Their World.* Tel-Aviv: Am Oved (in Hebrew).

Escobar, Arturo. 1991. "Anthropology and the Development Encounter: The Marketing of Development Anthropology." *American Ethnologist* 18(4):658–683.

Etzioni-Halevi, Hava, and Rina Shapira. 1977. *Political Culture in Israel: Cleavage and Integration among Israeli Jews.* New York: Praeger.

Even-Zohar, Itamar. 1981. "The Emergence of a Native-Hebrew Culture in Palestine: 1882–1948." *Studies in Zionism* 4:167–184.

Ewen, Stewart, and E. Ewen. 1979. *Channels of Desire: Mass Images and the Shaping of American Consciousness.* New York: McGraw-Hill.

Firer, Ruth. 1989. *Agents of Morality. [Sochnim Shel Halekach].* Hakibbutz Ha'meuhad (in Hebrew).

Fish, Stanley. 1980. *Is There a Text in This Class?—The Authority of Interpretive Communities.* Harvard: Harvard University Press.

Foucault, Michel. 1972. *The Archaeology of Knowledge and the Discourse on Language.* New York: Pantheon Books.

————. 1976. *The Archaeology of Knowledge.* New York: Harper and Row.

————. 1979. "What is an Author?" Trans. Kari Hanet, *Screen* 20(1), 13–33.

Friedman, Jonathan. 1994. *Cultural Identity and Global Process.* London: Sage.

————. 1992. "Myth, History and Political Identity." *Cultural Anthropology* 7: 194–210.

Frishman, Y. 1966. "We Shall Not Forget: Pupils' Impressions after Coming Back from Poland." The Ministry of Education, Jerusalem, pp. 9–11.

Furnham, Adrian, and Barrie Stacey. 1991. *Young People's Understanding of Society.* London: Routledge.

Gertz, Nurit. 1995. *Captive of a Dream: National Myths in Israeli Culture (Shevuya Bachaloma).* Tel-Aviv: Am-Oved (in Hebrew).

————. 1987. "The Company Was Walking." *Sratim* 3, April (in Hebrew).

Goldscheider, Calvin. 1996. *Israel's Changing Society: Population, Ethnicity, and Development.* Boulder, CO: Westview Press.

Goody, Jack. 1994. *The Culture of Flowers.* Cambridge: Cambridge University Press.

Gurevitch, Zali, and Gideon Aran. 1994a. "The Land of Israel: Myth and Phenomenon." In *Reshaping the Past: Jewish History and the Historians, Studies in Contemporary Jewry X.* pp. 195–210. Jerusalem: The Avraham Harman Institute of Contemporary Jewry.

————. 1994b. "Never in Place: Eliade and Judaic Sacred Space." *Arch. de Sc. Soc. des Rel* 87:135–152.

————. 1991. "On the Spot (Israeli Anthropology)." *Alpayim* 4:44–49 (in Hebrew).

Gutman, Israel, and Haim Shatzker. 1983. *Ha'shoah U'mashmauta* [The Holocaust and Its Meaning]. Mercaz Shazar: Jerusalem (in Hebrew).

Halbwachs, Morris. 1992 (1925). *On Collective Memory.* Chicago: The University of Chicago Press.

Handelman, Don. 1990. *Models and Mirrors: Towards an Anthropology of Public Events.* Cambridge: Cambridge University Press.

Handelman, Don, and Elihu Katz. 1990. "State Ceremonies of Israel—Remembrance Day and Independence Day." In Don Handelman (ed.), *Models and Mirrors*. Cambridge: Cambridge University Press.

Hannerz, Ulf. 1989. "Notes on the Global Ecumene." *Public Culture* 1(2):66–75.

Hazan, Haim. 1980. *The Limbo People: A Study of the Construction of the Time Universe Among the Aged*. London: Routledge and Kogan Paul.

———. 1990. *A Paradoxical Community: The Emergence of a Social World in an Urban Renewal Setting*. Greenwich, CT: JAI Press.

———. 1992. *Managing Change in Old Age*. Albany, New York: SUNY Press.

———. 1994. *Old Age: Construction and Deconstruction*. Cambridge: Cambridge University Press.

Heath, S. 1981. *Questions of Cinema*. Bloomington: University of Indiana Press.

Hebdige, D., and Hurd, G. 1978. "Reading and Realism." *Screen Education* 28:68–78.

Heilman, Samuel. 1983. *The People of the Book*. Chicago: Chicago University Press.

Helman, Sarit. 1993. "Refusal to Serve in the Army as an Attempt to Redefine Citizenship." Doctoral Thesis, The Hebrew University, Jerusalem (in Hebrew).

Herzog, Hanna, and Rina Shapira. 1986. "Will You Sign My Autograph Book? Using Autograph Books for a Sociohistorical Study of Youth and Social Frameworks." *Qualitative Sociology* 9 (2): 109–125.

Hoben, Allen. 1982. "Anthropologists and Development." *Annual Review of Anthropology* 11:349–375.

Holton, E. 1992. "The Cultic Roots of Culture." In *Theory of Culture,* Richard Munich and Neil Smesler (eds.), pp. 29–63. Berkeley: University of California Press.

Holub, Robert. 1984. *Reception Theory: A Critical Introduction*. London: Methuen.

Horowitz, Dan, and Baruch Kimmerling. 1974. "Some Social Implications of Military Service and the Reserve System in Israel." *Archives Europ enes de Sociologie* 15: 2652–2676.

Horowitz, Dan, and Moshe Lisak. 1977. *From Settlement to State*. Tel Aviv: Am Oved (in Hebrew).

———. 1978. *The Origins of the Israeli Polity*. Chicago: University of Chicago Press. International Committee on Project Renewal Evaluation.

———. 1981. "Guidelines for Evaluating Research." Jerusalem: The Jewish Agency for Israel.

Iser, Wolfgang. 1978. *The Act of Reading: A Theory of Aesthetic Response*. Baltimore, MD: The Johns Hopkins University Press.

Jameson, Fredrik. *Postmodernism, or, The Cultural Logic of Late Capitalism*. Durham: Duke University Press.

Van Mannen, J., P. Adler, and R. Adler (eds.). 1990. "Special Issue: The Presentation of Ethnographic Research." In *The Journal of Contemporary EthnographyI 19 (1)*. Newburry Park, CA: Sage.

Jowett, G.S. 1993. "Propaganda and the Gulf War." *Critical Studies in Mass Communication* 10.

Kantorowicz, E.H. 1957. *The King's Two Bodies*. Princeton: Princeton University Press.

Kapferer, Bruce. 1988. *Legends of People, Myths of State*. Washington, DC: Smithsonian Institution Press.

Katriel, Tamar. 1997. "Remaking Place: Cultural Production in Israeli Pioneer Settlement Museums." In *Grasping Land: Space and Place in Contemporary Israeli Discourse and Experience,* Eyal Ben-Ari and Yoram Bilu (eds.), pp. 146–177. Albany, New York: SUNY Press.

———. 1986. *Talking Straight: Dugri Speech in Israeli Sabra Culture.* Cambridge: Cambridge University Press.

———. 1987. "Rhetoric in Flames: Fire Inscriptions in Israeli Youth Movement Ceremonials." *Quarterly Journal of Speech* 73 (4), 444–459.

———. 1991. "Gibush: The Crystallization Metaphor in Israeli Cultural Semantics." In *Communal Webs: Culture and Communication in Israel, chap.* 2. Albany: SUNY Press.

Katz, Elihu, and Daniel Dayan. 1994. *Media Events.* Cambridge, Ma: Harvard University Press.

Katz, Elihu, and Michael Gurevitch. 1976. *The Secularization of Leisure: Culture and Communication in Israel.* Faber and Faber: London.

Kedourie, Elie. 1984. *The Crossman Confessions and Other Essays in Politics, History and Religion.* London: Mansel.

Keesing, R.M. 1974. "Theories of Culture." *Annual Review of Anthropology* 3:73–97.

Kellner, D.K. 1992. *The Persian Gulf TV War.* Boulder, CO: Westview Press.

Keren, M. 1995. *Professionals against Populism: The Peres Government and Politics.* Albany: State University of New York.

Kimmerling, Baruch. 1974. "Anomie and Integration in Israeli Society and the Salience of the Israeli-Arab Conflict." *Studies in Comparative International Development* 9(3): 64–89.

———. 1985. *The Interrupted System.* New Brunswick: Transaction Books.

———. 1989. "Boundaries and Frontiers of the Israeli Control System." In *The Israeli State and Society: Boundaries and Frontiers.* Baruch Kimmerling (ed.), pp. 265–284 Albany: SUNY Press.

———. 1992. "Sociology, Ideology, and Nation-Building: The Palestinians and Their Meaning in Israeli Sociology." *American Sociological Review* 57:446–460.

———. 1993. "Patterns of Militarism in Israel." *Archives Europeen de Sociologie* 34:196–223.

Kimmerling, Baruch, and Joel Migdal. 1992. *Palestinians: The Making of a People.* New York: The Free Press.

Kirschner, Susan. 1987. "'Then What have I to Do With Thee?': On Identity, Fieldwork, and Ethnographic Knowledge." *Cultural Anthropology* 2(2):211–234.

Klein, Uri, and Irma Klein. 1981. "We Simply Were in the Army Together." *Kolnoa (Cinema),* Summer Issue.

Kleinberger, Aharon Fritz. 1969. *Society, Schools and Progress in Israel.* Oxford: Pergamon Press.

Kuhn, Annette. 1982. *Women's Pictures, Feminism and Cinema.* London: Routledge.

Kunda, Gideon. 1992a. *Engineering Culture: Control and Commitment in a High-Tech Corporation.* Philadelphia: Temple, University Press.

———. 1992b. "Criticism on Probation: Ethnography and Cultural Critique in Israel." *Theoria U-bikoret* [Theory and Criticism] 2:7–24 (in Hebrew).

Lash, Scott, and John Urry. 1994. *Economies of Signs and Space.* London: Sage.

Levy, Amihay, Avi Bleich, and Eli Chen. 1987. "Israeli Adolescents and Military Service: Encounters." *Adolescence* 22, 88: 945–951.

Levy-Strauss, Claude. 1981. *The Naked Man: Introduction to the Science of Mythology.* London: Jonathan Cape.

Liebman, Charles, and Eliezer Don-Yehia. 1983. *Civil Religion in Israel: Traditional Judaism and Political Culture in the Jewish State.* Berkeley: UCLA Press.

Liebes, Tamar. 1992. "Decoding Television News: The Political Discourse of Israeli Hawks and Doves." *Theory and Society* 21:357–381.

Lieblich, Amia. 1995. *Studies in Psychology.* Jerusalem: Magnes Press.

Lifton, Robert Jay. 1977. "The Sense of Immortality: On Death and the Continuity of Life." In *Death in America, D.* Stannard (ed.). pp. 273–290. Philadelphia: University of Penn. Press.

———. 1979. *The Broken Connection: On Death and the Continuity of Life.* New York: Simon and Schuster.

———. 1986. *The Nazi Doctors.* New York: Basic Books.

Lissak, Moshe, and Dan Hurowitz. 1989. *Trouble in Utopia.* Albany: SUNY Press.

MacArthur, John R. 1992. *Second Front: Censorship and Propaganda in the Gulf War.* New York: Hill and Wang.

MacCabe, Colin. 1985. *Tracking the Signifier: Theoretical Essays in Film, Linguistics, Literature.* Minneapolis: University of Minnesota Press.

Manning, Peter, and Marcello Truzzi (eds). 1972. *Youth and Sociology.* New York: Prentice Hall.

Maoz, Azaria. 1988. *State Cults.* Beer-Sheba: Beer-Sheba University Press.

McGuigan, Jim. 1992. *Cultural Populism.* London and New York: Routledge.

Meron, Dan. 1992. *Opposite the Silent Brother: Studies in Poetry of the War of Independence (Mul Ha'ach Hashotek).* The Open University: Keter (in Hebrew).

Metz, Christiane. 1977. *The Imaginary Signifier: Psychoanalysis and the Cinema.* Trans. by C. Britton. Bloomington: Indiana University Press.

Morley, D. 1980. "Texts, Readers, Subjects." In *Culture, Media, Language.* Stuart Hall, D. Hobson, A. Lowe, and P. Willis (eds.), pp. 163–173. London: Hutchinson.

Mowlana, H., G. Gernber, and H. Schiller (eds.). 1992. *Triumph of the Image: The Media's War in the Persian Gulf—A Global Perspective.* Boulder, CO: Westview Press.

Morris, Benny. 1990. *1948 and After.* Oxford: The Clarendon Press.

Mosse, George. 1990. *Fallen Soldiers: Reshaping the Memory of the World Wars.* Oxford: Oxford University Press.

———. 1979. "National Cemeteries and National Revival: The Cult of the Fallen Soldiers in Germany." *Journal of Contemporary History* 14.

Mulvey, Laura. 1975. "Visual Pleasure and Narrative Cinema." *Screen* 16(3):6–18.

Myerhoff, Barbara. 1974. *Peyote Hunt: The Sacred Journey of the Hulchol Indians.* Ithaca: Cornell University Press.

Neeman, Y., and M. Zimmerman (eds.). 1987. *Introduction to Israeli Cinema.* A textbook. The Department of Cinema and Television, Tel Aviv University (in Hebrew).

Ofek, Hana. 1993. "The Integration of Renewal Neighborhoods into the Mainstream of Israeli Society: Illusion or Reality?" In *Local Communities and the Israeli Polity,* Efraim Ben-Zadok (ed.), pp. 123–155. Albany, NY: SUNY Press.

Olson, S.R. 1987. "Meta-Television: Popular Postmodernism." *Critical Studies in Mass Communication* 4:284–300.

Paine, Robert. 1983. "Israel and Totemic Time." *Rain* 59: 19–22.

Palgi, Yoel. 1978. *Ru'ach Gdola Ba'ah* [A Great Wind Is Coming]. Tel-Aviv: Am Oved (in Hebrew).

Pappe, Ilan. 1993. "The New History of the 1948 War." *Theory and Criticism* 3:99–114 (in Hebrew).

———. 1988. *The Making of the Arab-Israeli Conflict, 1947–1951.* St. Anthony's Macmillan Series, London.

———. (ed.). 1992 *Islam and Peace* Giv'at Haviva (in Hebrew).

Peled, Yoav. 1992. "Ethnic Democracy and the Legal Construction of Citizenship: Arab Citizens of the Jewish State." *American Political Science Review* 86(2):432–443.

Penley, C. 1989. *The Future of an Illusion: Film, Feminism, and Psychoanalysis.* Minneapolis: University of Minnesota Press.

Porat, Dina. 1986. *Leadership in Conflict—The Yishuv and the Holocaust 1942–45.* Am-Oved (in Hebrew).

Rabinowitz, Dan. 1997. *Overlooking Nazareth: The Ethnography of Exclusion in Galilee.* Cambridge Studies in Social and Cultural Anthropology. Cambridge: University of Cambridge Press.

Ram, Uri. 1994. *Israeli Society: Critical Aspects.* University of Haifa Press (in Hebrew).

———. 1989. "Civic Discourse in Israeli Sociological Thought." *International Journal of Politics, Culture and Society* 3(2):255–272.

Rapoport, Tamar. 1988. "Socialization Patterns in the Family, the School, and the Youth Movement." *Youth and Society* 20 (2): 159–179.

Rapoport, Tamar, Anat Penso, and Yoni Garb. 1994. "Contribution to the Collective by Religious-Zionist Adolescent Girls." *British Journal of Sociology of Education* 15 (3): 375–388.

Rapoport, Tamar, and Edna Lomsky-Feder. 1988. "Patterns of Transition to Adulthood: A Comparative Study of Israeli Society." *International Sociology* 3 (4): 415–432.

Raviv, Amiram, et al. 1998. "The Reaction of the Youth in Israel to the Assassination of Prime Minister Yitzhak Rabin." *Political Psychology* 19(2):255–277.

Raz, Aviad. 1994. "Rewriting the Holocaust: An Israeli Case Study in the Sociology of the Novel." In *Books on Israel,* vol. 3, chap. 1, a research annual, W. Zenner and R. Scott (eds.). Albany: State University of New York Press.

———. (ed.). 1995. "Zionism is Re-born in Auschwitz." Radio program transcript, 8 Aug., Galei-Zahal station (in Hebrew).

Regev, Motti. 1993. *Oud and Guitar: The Musical Culture of the Arabs in Israel.* Beit Berl: The Institute for Israeli-Arab Studies (in Hebrew).

Reich, A. 1972. "Changes and Developments in the Passover Haggadot of the Kibbutz Movement." Ph.D. dissertation, Texas University at Austin.

Ricoeur, Paul. 1991 (1986). *From Text to Action: Essays in Hermeneutics.* Evenston, Il.: Northwestern University Press.

Roniger, Luis, and Michael Feige. 1992. "From Pioneer to *Freier:* The Changing Models of Generalized Exchange in Israel." *Arch. Europ. Sociol.* 33: 280–307.

Rosaldo, Renato. 1987. "Where Objectivity Lies: The Rhetoric of Anthropology." In *The Rhetoric of the Human Sciences,* J. Nelson (ed.), pp. 87–109. Madison: Wisconsin University Press.

Rubinstein, Amnon. 1977. "The Rise and Fall of the Mythological Sabra." In *To Be a Free People,* Chap. 6. Tel Aviv: Shoken (in Hebrew).

Russcol, Herbert, and Margalit Banai. 1970. *The First Million Sabras: A Portrait of the Native Israelis.* New York: Hart.

Sa'adi, Ahmad. 1992. "Between State Ideology and Minority National Identity: Palestinians in Israel and in Israeli Social Science in Israel." *Review of Middle East Studies.* 5.

Said, Edward. 1978. *Orientalism.* London: Penguin Books.

Sanjek, Rojer. 1990. *Fieldnotes: The Makings of Anthropology.* Ithaca: Cornell University Press.

Schiller, H. 1992. "Manipulating Hearts and Minds." In *Triumph of the Image: The Media's War in The Persian Gulf—A Global Perspective,* Mowlana et al. (eds.). Boulder, CO: Westview Press.

Schneider, David. 1979. "Kinship, Community and Locality in American Culture." In *Kin and Communities,* A. J. Lichtman and J. R. Challmore (eds.). Washington DC: Smithsonian Institution.

Schneider, H. 1988. "Principles of Development: A View from Anthropology." In *Production and Autonomy: Anthropological Studies and Critiques of Development,* J. Bennet and J. Bowen (eds.), pp. 61–80. Lanham, MD: University Press of America.

Schwartz, Barry. 1982. "The Social Context of Commemoration: A Study in Collective Memory." *Social Forces* 61(2):374–462.

Segev, Tom. 1991. *The Seventh Million.* London: Maxwell-Macmillan.

Sered, Susan. 1991. "Gender, Immanence and Transcendence: The Candle-Lighting Repertoire of Middle-Eastern Jews." *Metaphor and Symbolic Activity* 6:293–304.

Shafir, Gershon. 1989. *Land, Labor, and the Israeli-Palestinian Conflict.* Cambridge: Cambridge University Press.

Shaham, Natan, and Tsvi Ra'anan (eds.). 1991. *War in the Gulf: Collection of Essays.* Tel Aviv: Sifriat Poalim (in Hebrew).

Shalev, Michael. 1992. *Labour and the Political Economy in Israel.* Oxford: Oxford University Press.

Shamgar-Handelman, Lea. 1991. "Celebration of Bureucracy: Brithday Parties in Israeli Kindergartens" *Ethnology,* 30: 293–315.

Shamgar-Handelman, Lea, and Don Handelman. 1989. "Holiday Celebrations in Israeli Kindergartens: Relationships between Representations of Collectivity and Family in the Nation-State." In *Education in Comparative Context,* E. Krausz (ed.), pp. 412–444. New Brunswick, NJ: Transaction Books.

Shapira, Anita. 1990. "A Generation of the Land (*Dor Ba'arretz*)" *Alapayim* 2:178–203 (in Hebrew).

Shapira, Rina, and Rachel Peleg. 1984. "From Blue Shirt to White Collar." *Youth and Society* 16(2): 195–216.

Shapiro, Yonatan. 1978. *Democracy in Israel.* Tel-Aviv: Massada (in Hebrew).

Shilling, Chris. 1993. *The Body and Social Theory.* London: Sage.

Shils, Edward. 1975. *Center and Periphery.* Chicago: University of Chicago Press.

Shlaim, Avi. 1990. *The Politics of Partition.* Oxford: Oxford University Press.

Shokeid, M. 1990. *Children of Circumstances.* Ithaca: Cornell University Press.

———. 1992. "Commitment and Contextual Study in Anthropology." *Cultural Anthropology* 7:464–477.

Silverman, Kaja. 1988. *The Acoustic Mirror: The Female Voice in Psychoanalysis and Cinema.* Bloomington: University of Indiana Press.

Sivan, Emmanuel. 1991. *The 1948 Generation: Myth, Profile and Memory.* Ma'arachot—IDF Publishing House, Israel: The Ministry of Defense (in Hebrew).

Smooha, Sami. 1978. *Israel: Pluralism and Conflict.* Berkeley: University of California Press.

———. 1990. *Arabs and Jews in Israel: Conflicting and Shared Attitudes in a Divided Society.,* vol. 1, Boulder, CO: Westview Press.

———. 1992. *Arabs and Jews in Israel.* Boulder: Westview Press.

Stacy, M. 1969. "The Myth of Community Studies." *British Journal of Sociology* 20:134–147.

Stern, M. 1992. "Reflections on the Gulf War." *Sichot* [Conversations]: *The Israeli Journal of Psychotherapy* 7(1) (in Hebrew).

Sternhell, Ze'ev. 1995. *Nation-Building or a New Society?* Tel-Aviv: Am Oved (in Hebrew).

Stevens, T. 1978. "Reading the Realist Film." *Screen Education* 26:13–34.

Swirski, Shlomo. 1981. *Orientals and Ashkenazim in Israel: The Ethnic Division of Labor.* Haifa: Machbarot for Research and Criticism (in Hebrew).

Synnott, Anthony. 1995. *The Body Social: Symbolism, Self and Society.* London: Routledge.

Taylor, Phillip M. 1992. *War and the Media: Propaganda and Persuasion in the Gulf War.* Manchester, England: Manchester University Press.

Taub, Gadi. 1997. *A Dispirited Rebellion: Essays on Contemporary Israeli Culture (Ha'Mered Ha'shfuf: Al Tarbut Tzeira Be'Yisrael).* Tel-Aviv: Ha'kibbutz Ha'meuchad (in Hebrew).

Turner, Victor. 1969. *The Ritual Process—Structure and Anti-Structure.* Chicago: Aldine.

———. 1976. "Social Dramas and Ritual Metaphors." *In Ritual, Play and Performance,* R. Shechner and N. Schuman (eds.). New York: Seabury Press.

———. 1977. "Variations on a Theme on Liminality." In *Secular Ritual,* S.F. Moore and B. Myerhoff (eds.), Amsterdam: Assen, Van Gorcum.

Turner, V., and Edith Turner. 1978. *Image and Pilgrimage in Christian Culture.* New York: Columbia University Press.

Tyler, Stephen A. 1987. *The Unspeakable: Discourse, Dialogue, and Rhetoric in the Postmodern World.* Madison: University of Wisconsin Press.

Van Gennep, Arnold. 1969 (1908). *The Rites of Passage.* Translated by M. B. Visedom and G. L. Caffee, Chicago, University of Chicago Press, Phoenix Books.

Van-Toeffelen, T. 1978. "The Manchester School in Africa and Israel: A Critique." *Dialectical Anthropology* 3:67–83.

Vardi, Ronit. 1989. *The Mark Bearers: Dialogues with Second Generation Israelis.* Keter Publications (in Hebrew).

Waagenaar, Sam. 1960. *Women of Israel.* Tel-Aviv: Lonnie Kahn and Co.

Wallerstein, Immanuel. 1974. *The Modern World System.* New York: Academic Press.

Wagner, R. 1986. *Symbols that Stand for Themselves.* Chicago: University of Chicago Press.

Waugh, Patricia. 1984. *Metafiction: The Theory and Practice of Self-Conscious Fiction.* New York: Methuen.

Weisbrod, L. 1982. "*Gush Emunim* Ideology: From Religious Doctrine to Political Action." *Middle Eastern Studies* 18: 265–275.

Werman, Robert. 1993. *Notes from a Sealed Room: An Israeli View of the Gulf War.* Carbondale and Edwardsville: Southern Illinois University Press.

Warren, R. 1973. *The Community in America.* Chicago: Rand McNally.

Weil, Shalva. 1986. "The Language and Ritual of Socialization: Birthday Parties in a Kindergarten Context." *MAN* 21:329–341.

Wistrich, Robert, and David Ohana. 1995. *Myth and History.* London:

Yishai, Yael. 1987. *Interest Groups in Israel: The Test of Democracy.* Tel-Aviv: Am-Oved (in Hebrew).

Young, James E. 1988. *Writing and Rewriting the Holocaust.* Bloomington: Indiana University Press.

————. 1991. *Writing and Rewriting the Holocaust: Narrative and the Consequences of Interpretation*. Bloomington: Indiana University Press.

Yuchtman-Yaar, Ephraim. 1998. "Values and Attitudes of Jewish and Israeli Youth in Israel's 50 Anniversary." Paper presented at the conference "Between Masada and Go'a," Tel-Aviv, 17 June (in Hebrew).

Yuchtman-Yaar, Ephraim, Yohanan Peres, and D. Goldberg. 1994. "Doing Research Under Missiles: Israeli Morale During the Gulf War." Unpublished paper, Department of Sociology, Tel-Aviv University.

Yuchtman-Yaar, Ephraim, et al. 1998. Personal, Social and National Attitudes of Israeli Youth in the Anniversary Year. Published by the Israeli Institute for Economic and Social Research, Tel-Aviv (in Hebrew).

Zerubavel, Yael. 1980. "The Last Stand: The Transformations of Symbols in Modern Israel." Ph.D. dissertation, at University of Pennsylvania: Philadelphia.

————. 1990. "The Historic, the Legendary, and the Incredible: Invented Tradition and Collective Memory in Israel." In *Commemorations: The Politics of National Identity*, J. Gillis (ed.), pp. 105–270, Princeton, N.J.: Princeton University Press.

————. 1991. "New Beginnings, Old Past: The Collective Memory of Pioneering in Israeli Culture." In *New Perspectives on Israeli History: The Early Years of the State*, L. Silberstein (ed.), pp. 193–215. New York: New York University Press.

————. 1995. *Recovered Roots*. Albany, NY: State University of New York Press.

Zukerman, Moshe. 1988–89. "The Curse of Forgetting: Israel and the Holocaust." *Telos* 78:43–54.

————. 1993. *Shoah in the Sealed Room: "The Holocaust" in Israeli Press during the Gulf War* (in Hebrew).

INDEX

Index